Flying Thru Life:

How to Grow Your Business and Relationships with Applied Spirituality

My Soulrific Journey to Abundance and Ease

Dedication

If there were ever was a person in this lifetime who has helped me find my wings, take flight and soar it would be Susan "PC" Gilbert. She has been a friend across the ages, and has introduced me to my three life passions: flying, small business and spirituality. These have been delicately woven together, and are the heart and soul of this book. Susan lovingly encouraged, nudged and elevated me while demonstrating the patience of an angel. When I dreamed as impossibly big as my heart would allow she opened it even wider than I could have ever imagined.

I dedicate this book to you, Susan, and my hope and prayer is that it changes the world the same way you have forever changed mine.

"Entrepreneurship is about turning what excited you in life into capital, so that you can do more of it and move forward with it."

~Richard Branson Founder of Virgin Group

Contents

Introduction

One of my friends once referred to me as "Bobby D Steamroller"—and as much as it embarrasses me now, her description was right on. Back then, many of my business transactions ended with a threat of litigation, letters from an attorney, or a lawsuit. I was constantly evicting people, and I remember once bragging about winning in small claims court three times that week. I didn't consider anything a victory unless it was an unconditional surrender and I got everything I wanted—including the shoes on their feet. I had a powerful reputation for going for the jugular in every business transaction.

Here's how it used to go down. Arriving in my exotic car with my attorney in tow, I'd make it clear right up front that if we didn't settle on *my* terms, we would go to war. I intentionally created pain, fear, and chaos so that the other guy was so intimidated and overwhelmed that he'd settle on the lowest possible price just to stop the pain. And if things didn't move along as quickly as I thought they should, I'd start screaming as loud as I could. My heart would pound, my face would turn beet red, and I'd start shaking. It worked simply because it was terrifying.

Of course, saying it worked isn't really what happened. I never seemed to work out a deal twice with any one person; no one wanted to face *that* a second time. I experienced horrific turnover among my employees and independent contractors. And even when those people stayed around, they got back at me passively through low productivity or employee theft.

Sounds like exactly the kind of guy you want to do business with, right?

Thankfully, I'm not that way anymore. In fact, I'm the polar opposite. I discovered the power of putting some specific principles to work, and my business has *tripled* since that day. My life has been easier, not more difficult. People enjoy working with me. I have lots of people I now consider partners because we accomplish many deals working *together*. When I walk away from a deal today, I have the satisfaction of knowing that everyone won. And I'm going to teach you exactly how to arrive at that place yourself.

This book was conceived as I flew myself to more than thirty countries during the past three years. Flying over the polar ice cap alone at twenty-three thousand feet and at 230 miles per hour wearing a survival suit isn't what you think of as the typical business classroom environment, but it taught me some of the most profound lessons of my life. I'm going to share those lessons with you. I'm going to teach you how to achieve business success and personal abundance without the pain you may think is necessary.

Don't worry—I'm not one of those guys with a big cheesy smile who shows up in a $1,600 suit and waves his arms in the air in front of a dazzling multimedia presentation, all for the astronomical price of your admission ticket. Quite the opposite: I'm not in this for the money. I'm in it to give back. (I'm not taking a profit from this book or from my website; any money from these not-for-profit ventures will be used to help distribute these principles to as many people as possible.) Nor am I a guy who spouts off stuff I've never actually tried. What you're about to read is what I learned firsthand and what I've practiced firsthand. It's what brought me to a place of peace and success from the place of pain where I used to be.

You know all about that pain. You and I were taught that business and personal success requires suffering. If you want to get ahead, you have to sacrifice, work longer hours, make more calls, stay later, and do things you don't want to do—maybe even violating your integrity or doing things that aren't best for everyone. If you could just do all that, you've been told, you could finally make enough money. Then you'd finally be happy.

But what if that doesn't work? The scary truth is, it often doesn't. Then what happens? You feel out of control. Frightened. Self-doubt bubbles to the surface. And the little voice inside your head labels you a loser. You can't figure out how all that happened because you've worked as hard as you possibly can. No one could have expected more.

I know. I've been there. I've had to battle with that same voice inside *my* head. But then I discovered a connection to Spirit, and all that changed. It can change for you too.

I'm not talking any specific form of religion or spirituality. That is your own journey if you choose to take it. Instead, I intend to share some spiritual principles and practices that will help you live your life more fully and abundantly—and that includes your business life. I will show you how much easier and more pleasant and more profitable you can be when you swim *with* the current instead of against it.

I thought about choosing a title for this book that was more mass-market or mainstream oriented. Instead, I chose Flying Thru Life because that name personifies for me the desired outcome. When I partnered with Spirit in my business and my life, I made a soul connection that created a terrific change in my life – a soulrific change. I also want what I am about to share to be fun for you to read—and I hope it elicits a feeling of surprise and wonder at what is possible and attainable for you.

This book is written for you, the person who has a full, busy life. It's a quick, easy read; you can read it on a plane or while you stand in line at the post office. I want you to look at it as a blueprint in guiding you as you make changes that will result in more abundance, greater pleasure, fuller joy, and more meaningful connections in your personal life.

Please understand that reading this book is just the beginning. This process is experiential. If you are to make real changes in your life, you must practice these principles. I hope as you do that you will share your successes with the rest of us at www.flyingthrulife.com. We are all connected, and all of us can benefit from the experiences you have and the growth you achieve—just as you will benefit from what we experience as we learn our lessons together.

"You are always free to change your mind and choose a different future, or a different past."

~Richard Bach

Chapter 1

Setting the Stage: My Story

My freshman year at USC, I was a skinny kid who had few social graces—but I did have zits, braces on my teeth, and a head full of unkempt hair. I didn't even know hair mousse or gel existed; I had no game and no success with the ladies. I never thought of myself as smart, but I worked hard to overcome that in school. I remember repeating my personal mantra—*body, mind, soul*—over and over again, reminding myself that my physical challenges didn't totally define me.

I struggled through those years at USC. I had nobody to mentor me, and I learned everything by trial and error. Mostly error. But I eventually got the coveted degree: In 1988, I graduated with a bachelor of science degree in accounting from USC.

After graduation, my father persuaded me to join the Navy. By then I was at least a little bit cool—I finally had a car, some of my own money, and a respectable job. A few months later all that didn't matter: the Gulf

War broke out in earnest. I had one choice: I could be stationed on the East Coast or the West Coast of the United States. I was no dummy: I chose the West Coast because I'd heard that the ships on the East Coast were being sent to the Persian Gulf. I was wrong. Turns out *all* ships were being sent to the gulf.

As a twenty-five-year-old naval officer in the first Gulf War, I learned how hard the world could be. I was on a forty-year-old steam cruiser that was loaded with more weapons and technology than I had ever seen in one place—and the ship wasn't originally designed for all those weapon systems. That's not all: it didn't carry enough people to support them. Life became very challenging, a classic case of adding more rats to a cage until they start eating each other.

I've never worked harder at a job with so little success. I was using the management style we were all taught: yelling, screaming, and being a general hard-ass. I was pushing these guys as hard as I could because I wanted to show the world how much I could accomplish. This was my first test, and I didn't intend to fail.

This style of doing business didn't go over well with the enlisted guys who got paid the same whether they worked or simply sat around. I pushed my first-class petty officer so hard that he broke down in tears in front of the master chief of the command and kicked a garbage can across the office in a moment of frustration. I was told on more than one occasion not to go topside at night because if you were pushed overboard by an enlisted guy, they would never find your body.

On one occasion I was waiting to talk to the chief engineer, a big, stereotypical New Yorker. Two guys went in ahead of me, and I could hear him berating them at the top of his lungs. When it was my turn, he screamed at me so loudly that he sprayed spit all over my face while I stood at attention. Terrified, humiliated, and grossed out beyond words, I decided I would do whatever it took to get out of the Navy as quickly as I could.

The program I got my commission under allowed me to transfer into the reserves as soon as I got qualified at a particular level. My intention was to qualify, obtain written proof of my qualification, and give everyone on the ship the finger as I walked over the brow better than a year before they deployed to the Middle East. The qualification process normally took about two years, but I was ready to take the board after about a year—the fastest anyone had done so in the forty-year history of the ship. Life was good and I was about to earn my freedom in the most dramatic way possible.

To my utter dismay, my board was cancelled the morning I was scheduled to take it. The executive officer said I needed more experience on the bridge, even though I was his best ship driver.

Six months later, I was scheduled to take the board, which would get me off the ship the day before it deployed. I thought I was the only one who realized my fortunate timing—but one of the chief warrant officers tipped-off the executive officer. My board was cancelled a second time just twenty-four hours prior to

a six-month deployment. Needless to say, I was pissed beyond words as I tried to prepare in just twenty-four hours for being away for six months.

The stress of war was brutal; we all lived on adrenaline and were far from happy. It affected people at all levels; the chief engineer on another ship had a breakdown and was relieved of his position. We paid a huge price in terms of the quality of our lives.

Unfortunately, I learned some bad lessons that would later impact all aspects of my life. One was my overly aggressive, in-your-face way of doing business. But I was also taught a valuable lesson, though it took me years to understand: fighting, in any aspect of life, is a huge waste of energy.

As soon as my tour was finished, I got out of active duty and joined the Navy Reserve for ten years. I landed a job at the corrupt and now-defunct Arthur Andersen, the largest accounting and consulting firm in the world at the time. I didn't enjoy corporate America. I remember waking each day and not wanting to get out of the shower. I was diligently following in my father's footsteps, still trying to please him after all these years, but feeling that I was working long hours only to make greedy partners richer. It was hard to force a smile on my face every day and do something that I was not passionate about.

I kept hearing people say, "Do something you are passionate about and the money will come." I didn't believe that would work. But in reality, I just didn't know what I was passionate about.

While at Arthur Andersen, I bought a 1971 Pantera Detomaso, a car considered the poor man's exotic. Nobody could figure out how a lowly staff auditor could afford such a car. Here's how: I found a plumber whose business was imploding and made him a ridiculous cash offer. When he accepted it, I took a $14,000 advance on my credit card and showed up with a cashier's check.

All the auditors drove Honda Acuras; the partners had the slightly more expensive Legend. I didn't care that I was disrupting the establishment—I was intent on being me. I would pull up to a job site, my four-hundred-horsepower engine racing, the four exhaust pipes blasting away. I remember the windows of the office building vibrating as I was parked and all the employees racing to the windows to see what the hell all the racket was. I'd get out and saunter into the office like it was no big deal. I pissed a lot of people off in those days, and I honestly didn't care.

Not surprisingly, I was fired from Arthur Andersen just shy of my second year there. Apparently, the managing partner could see that my heart wasn't in it. As I walked out of the office with my box of personal belongings, one of my former managers asked how I was doing. I let him know I had just been fired. He said something I will never forget: "They just did you the biggest favor of your life; you just don't know it yet."

I lay on my bed later that day, crying like a little child, feeling lost, hopeless, humiliated. I wanted to punch the guy who fired me in his smug little face. How was I going to make my mortgage payment? How had

I gotten myself into this situation, and why was the world picking on me? My plans for making it big as a fortune 500 chief financial officer—like my father—had just been flushed down the toilet. I remember in that moment making a promise to God that shocked me: "God, if you get me out of this situation, I will dedicate my life to you." I had no idea what that meant at the time; I only felt hurt, scared, and afraid.

The next day, I realized I had just given my entire pathetic life away to God. Later, I wondered if the contract was valid, since it had been made under duress and seemed a bit dramatic. Here I was, trying to weasel my way out of a verbal contract with God. Wasn't it only the Pope who could make deals like this? As it turns out, it would take me twenty years to begin to fulfill this promise to God, but it *was* fulfilled. And it changed my life.

But I'm getting ahead of myself.

Since I really hated working in corporate America, I didn't know what to do next. The thought of working hard for someone else did not excite me. I certainly didn't want to give my life to some ungrateful company and be worn out by the time I retired with little to show for it. I knew too many people like that. So, giving the finger to my father's dreams of me being a big-shot corporate guy, I took a six-month set of orders in the Navy. I eventually served another twelve years of active and reserve time.

During that time, I started a couple of small businesses with the help of my partner and now publisher/

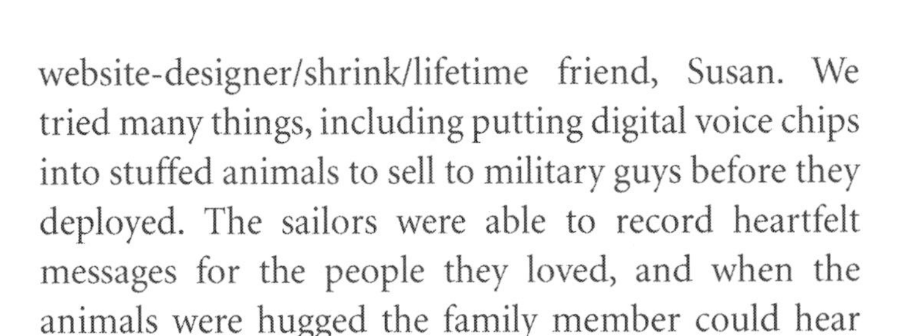

website-designer/shrink/lifetime friend, Susan. We tried many things, including putting digital voice chips into stuffed animals to sell to military guys before they deployed. The sailors were able to record heartfelt messages for the people they loved, and when the animals were hugged the family member could hear the message that had been recorded for them.

"Talking Creatures" gave me my first shot at greatness when I got the attention of the buyer for the entire West Coast of the United States; he asked me to come in the next day and sign a contract to have the stuffed animals at every exchange in his territory. That morning he called and cancelled. I had mentioned what I was doing to our stuffed-animal supplier, and the supplier had taken our client. Game over. To make matters worse, our competitor's product was junkier than ours, and the batteries died on the shelf. After that bad experience, the buyer had to discount the price of the products to unload the thousands he had purchased. He never wanted to see another talking animal in his life.

We also had some success in Southern California with a business we named "New Looks on Video." We superimposed various hairstyles and colors onto video images of people's faces, setting up events in cosmetic departments and selling the imaging service at a reduced price if customers bought a certain amount of product. This worked well for a time and doubled or tripled the cosmetic line's business for the day if the event was properly promoted. We also did trade-show events as well, drawing huge crowds of people to

the booths. The hair-imaging business eventually split up—or blew up—depending how you looked at it.

After a difficult business breakup, I went out on my own and started buying rental properties. I renovated at night and on weekends and found great joy in working with my hands, being on my own, and breathing new life and love into the old, neglected buildings I bought at substantial discounts. I installed inexpensive wood floors I bought at Home Depot, along with new white blinds and baseboards. I textured the walls with a five-dollar box of topping mix, and for the grand finale, I painted the walls my signature color, Swiss Mocha. I felt like an artist, and these units were my canvasses.

The San Diego real estate market was increasing 22 to 32 percent a year, something that would continue for the next eleven years. The money was easy to get too; I'd heard that if you could fog a mirror you could get a loan. I fogged many mirrors using cash advances from my credit cards as down payments. For the first time in my life, it seemed that my interests, skill set, and the universe were in alignment. I foolishly thought that nothing could slow me down—and that at this rate I would surely be a billionaire within a few years.

As it turns out, I had some valuable lessons to learn.

I had been told by my mortgage broker that the most units any landlord could accumulate without help from other sources was a hundred. Over the next nineteen years, I accumulated a little more than a hundred rental units on fourteen properties. Getting to that number wasn't easy, and it was a struggle to reach that goal by age forty-four. The numbers on my résumé were impressive, but the methods I used to get there were not: I had paid with others' blood, sweat, and tears, leaving behind a trail of wrecked relationships, bad feelings, and poor business practices.

My success had taken a toll on me. I was tired and angry, rarely (if ever) trusted anyone, and was overly intense, difficult to be around, ego driven and pushing everyone's limits. I thought that the fastest way between two points was over the top of someone. And that's the person I described in the introduction to this book—Bobby D Steamroller.

At that time, my past business partner said something I'd misinterpreted as a compliment—she said she didn't know anyone who was willing to give up more to get ahead than I was.

Although I didn't realize it at the time, she was teaching me several critical lessons. First, I was trying to define myself with wealth. My total focus was on making as much money as I could and acquiring as many properties as fast as I could. It was all "goal-line" stuff—more properties, faster cars, better clothes, more hot women. The only god I worshipped was the money god.

And the second lesson was even more critical: I was willing to give up everything to get the "goal-line" stuff. I was willing to give up my health, my friends, my other relationships, my integrity, and even my soul. I cared little for my fellow man—unless, of course, they could help me get ahead. I was lost. And it would take some

time before I even realized it.

The economy slowed, and so did my business. I needed capital to grow, but banks were tightening up on lending. If I wanted to grow, I needed to find a new source of funding. Asking people for money seemed terrifying and humiliating to me. I didn't want to be seen as a beggar. I was too proud for that. I knew that to ask someone for money would put them in the power position, and that didn't feel good to me. I was used to being in control, even though all I'd really had was the illusion of control.

I looked for an easier way.

What I found was the Entrepreneurs Organization; its members mostly partied and went on guy trips, but they occasionally had lectures and a forum where a bunch of men sat around a table discussing their business and sometimes personal challenges. It was a good process, but progress was painfully slow. Frustrated by the lack of movement, I hired a personal business coach for two hours once a month, and we were able to clear an issue after about three months. But I wanted to move more quickly through my issues—at that pace it would take forever, and I needed help now!

Little did I know that help was accessible to me *right then*—and had always been. Just as it's accessible to you. And it's simpler than you'd ever guess.

"The most difficult thing is the decision to act, the rest is merely tenacity. The fears are paper tigers. You can do anything you decide to do. You can act to change and control your life; and the procedure, the process is its own reward."

~ *Amelia Earhart*

Chapter 2

The Help You Need: What's Holding You Back Is YOU

While I was trying to discover how to get what I needed, I had a profound download from Spirit: **it was ME who was holding ME back.**

Put another way, "Outer experience is a reflection of inner reality." In other words, any turmoil or issues we are experiencing in our outer world are a reflection of what is going on inside of us. If we want the world to change, we must first change what's going on inside of us.

I had enough business skills. I had studied hard enough. I had gotten the grades I needed. I had gone to a good school. I didn't need to go back to business school or get out my old college textbooks. I didn't need to attend a seminar on making more sales or raising capital. I didn't need to spill my guts at the entrepreneur forum. I needed to work on me!

If I wanted more of anything in this world, I had to get out of the way and change the way I was showing up in the world. I had to let go of my anger. I had to find a way of doing things that would let everyone win. I had to get in alignment with spirit (God, the Universe, whatever you choose to call it). I needed to go with the current and not against it.

So you can see how this works, I want you to imagine putting on a backpack. Now imagine that every bad habit, bad practice, unfair dealing, impure motive, lack of integrity—whatever problem you're trying to solve—is a good-sized rock. Those rocks are piled up at your feet. Now, one at a time, put those rocks in your backpack. At first it's no big deal. Okay, it's a little heavy, but certainly not what you'd consider a handicap. Oh, but wait: The more rocks you pile into that backpack, the more impossible you find it to move ahead—to take even a few steps—without great and literally backbreaking effort. In my case, my backpack was filled with boulders, and I had to free myself of those boulders. I had to get rid of what was holding me back and slowing me down.

Here's another example that will help you see what I'm talking about. You've probably flown in a storm before. Remember taking off? You may recall being bumped around a little in the moisture and turbulence. But once the pilot breaks through the clouds and reaches flying altitude, everything is incredibly bright and clear. You can see for miles, and it is absolutely beautiful. All the hard work (and fuel) to get to that altitude is worth it, and you are about to experience cool, smooth, clear air ahead!

Once I realized I had to change myself, the Universe complied by putting six people in front of me who had graduated from a program at the University of Santa Monica (where I would eventually get my graduate degree in spiritual psychology with an emphasis in consciousness health and healing, a program specialized on heart-centered learning that would profoundly impact my business and my life). These people all confirmed what I had come to realize: I needed to work on myself first.

As you already know, I was focused on the goal-line stuff. And you already know your own goal-line stuff—accomplishments, clothes, houses, cars, people to date, money in the bank, promotions at work. If you're looking at a chart that graphs your growth, the goal-line stuff would be graphed along the horizontal axis. That's because acquiring more "stuff" might make you happy for a time, but the satisfaction doesn't last for long. And goal-line growth is dependent on things—things you acquire, things you accumulate.

At the opposite is soul-line growth. It's charted on the vertical axis, and it depends entirely on you. Only *you* can move yourself along the soul line. Soul-line growth is related to your spiritual evolution, and you grow along the soul line through meditation, selfless service, and working your process. As you grow and become more aware of your connection with Spirit, it allows the ever-present joy within you to flourish. Removing the filters of personal issues that cloud your awareness of this inner bliss, it enables you to be more compassionate toward yourself and others.

The pleasant surprise in all this is that as you move ahead on the soul line, it helps you accomplish more of what you want on the goal line—and in record time.

Now that you have a framework on which to build, it's time to explore Spirit.

What *is* Spirit?

Spirit is found in silence, gratitude, oneness, intuition, integrity, and compassion. You connect with Spirit when you remove filters, engage in authentic communication, clear incomplete cycles of action, set intentions, take full responsibility, reframe, connect with the collective consciousness, and are impeccable with your word. When you use the Spirit through these principles and practices, *you will achieve things in your personal and business life you never thought possible.* You don't need to know the *how*. Spirit already knows *how*. And since all knowledge comes from the collective conscious and Spirit, all you need to do is tap into it.

With the help of Spirit, you can reach your goals and have an abundant life. *You simply achieve more when you are in alignment with Spirit.* I know because it has happened to me, as you'll see throughout the rest of this book. The good news is, you don't have to work yourself to death in the process. You do it by cocreating with Spirit.

You're no different than everyone else: You could use some help. Spirit is right there, waiting to assist you. Accessing Spirit won't cost you anything except a change in the way you see the world. And the help isn't limited—you have an all-knowing business consultant and partner available to you twenty-four hours a day. Best of all? He can play the entire game without ever getting tired.

Going back to something I mentioned earlier, using Spirit is the difference between swimming with the current and fighting against it. Nobody is strong enough to swim against a strong current for very long. You may be successful for a time, as I was, but swimming against the current takes a toll on you, and chances are you won't get far. You are fighting the lessons the Universe has for you, and it's not a fight you can win because the Universe keeps coming back stronger. It's like stepping into the ring with a prizefighter. You might be able to win one round, but not two or three in a row.

Before I move on to the specifics, I need to explain that I am introducing various concepts of spirituality in this book. Spirituality can include things like reading, meditating, studying, counseling, and listening for and following divine guidance. But please understand that taken alone, spirituality is not enough. Relying only on spirituality would be like trying to sit on a one-legged stool. In every decision you make, you must also consider wisdom and experience. That's why I'm sharing my own stories with you—they incorporate twenty-four years of experience in real estate, four years of flying as a general aviation pilot, fourteen years of military service, and my brief stint in corporate America, with all the wisdom I gained along the way. I intend to share with you both my perceived successes *and my failures* because they are all relevant

to growth and spiritual evolution. And along with that, I will share all the things I've done personally to make personal and business growth happen in my life.

Best of all, you can learn—and practice—these lessons anytime, anywhere.

You are in charge. *You* are the one who will make it happen because you are the only one who can seek and remove the barriers you have built against the peace, healing, and growth that is possible for you.

It is my goal that we see the challenges in our daily lives not as some form of cosmic torture but rather as opportunities to heal what we have been carrying with us so we can more fully express the joy that has always been a part of us.

"The real voyage of discovery consists not in seeking new landscapes, but in having new eyes."

~ *Marcel Proust*

Chapter 3

Authentic Communication: Speaking from Your Heart

I had completed my first year at USM and was intellectually learning spiritual psychology and its principles. The property management company I own was considering an upgrade to our software from the Excel spreadsheets I had created fifteen years earlier to the latest, greatest integrated real-estate software package on the market. The software was expensive, and none of us had a clue how to operate it. I knew shifting over to the new software would be a time-consuming process, but I decided it would be worth it.

After a few months of fumbling along, we hit a wall we could not get around. Several of the software's essential functions weren't working properly. As it turns out, when we had provided our list of properties to the software company, we'd provided the addresses we used in a format the software couldn't recognize. What we thought was a minor issue was actually a

major issue and was going to take several hours of someone's time to resolve—at a rate of $200 per hour.

I called the software manufacturer and eventually worked my way up the chain until I was talking to the president. She was firm on her position to charge us. After all, it was our error, she said. We had provided addresses in the wrong format. I didn't think we should be responsible for the cost of the repair because no one had told us in what format the software needed the addresses. Our conversation was rising in intensity as we both repeatedly presented our best arguments. Neither one of us was listening to the other because each of us was busy trying to decide what to say next. Tempers flared. The conversation got heated. I did my very best to bully her, but it wasn't working. Then I insinuated that perhaps it was time to get an attorney involved.

The other end of the phone went silent. During the long pause, I realized I had just pushed this other ego-driven person too far, and anything that was said from this point would be fodder for a lawsuit.

Sure enough, she responded by saying, "If a lawsuit is threatened, I can't say anything further."

We had gone from zero to a hundred in just a few minutes. And both of us were polishing our canons for a full-blown attack—each just waiting to see who would pull the trigger first.

I had visions of sending $600 letters between attorneys and then paying more for the hours they spent reviewing the case in excruciating detail over the next several months as we both got our legal counsels up to speed. I knew the end result would be each of us paying the attorneys thousands and thousands of dollars before going our separate ways. Moreover, all the time we spent getting the data into the new software would amount to a huge waste of time, and we would go back to our old-school way of doing business with Excel spreadsheets. I knew I would be pissed about this event for years to come.

What happened next would have astonished the people who knew me best.

I leaned back in my chair in front of a window that overlooked the San Diego Bay from my ridiculously large custom-made mahogany desk, and I took a very deep breath. I decided there had to be a better way to spend my time than fighting with another type-A, ego-driven person. I knew I had the skills to handle this situation, and it was time for some *authentic communication.*

I made my voice as calm as I could and said, "Karen Ann, the truth is, I haven't sued anybody in years, and I don't intend to sue you. My girls love using your software and tell me how fun it's been learning the different modules. But right now, we are scared. I am hemorrhaging cash, and we don't know what to do. We desperately, desperately need your help."

Once again her end of the line went silent. After a few moments, she said she would get back to me. About thirty minutes later my phone rang. The software company's chief information officer told me he had three coders sitting next to him and that together we were going to resolve this problem right there and then. As we identified the issues, he handed them off one at a time to the coders. He even handled a couple of the issues himself.

We had the issue resolved within thirty minutes. The last question the chief information officer asked me was concerned with how I was going to spend my weekend. I had made a friend in the midst of all this. The problem was solved, and the attorneys hadn't gotten a penny! I didn't need to go to war. I made one more call that day to Karen Ann and said six words: "Thank you, thank you, thank you!"

As I hung up the phone, I was still trying to comprehend what had just transpired. I had taken a new route, and the scenery was totally different. I had gotten altitude and bypassed the frustration and anger I would normally have experienced, thanks to the power of the spiritual principles and practices I'd learned. And flying through life at this higher altitude was not only much more direct but much more pleasant—I didn't get bumped around in the turbulence I always found at lower altitudes. I was on autopilot and had a tailwind pushing me along at 265 miles per hour.

This new way of being had proven its value in my life. I had just created a new business model. I'd moved from adversarial to humane. I had saved thousands of dollars, months of time and frustration, and my business began operating at the level of efficiency we needed. I realized that I had the power to choose love and compassion anytime I wanted over conflict, anger, and separation. I could take a situation fraught with conflict, ego, and low vibrations of energy and transform it into a spiritual way to connect with another person. I could share my feelings and not be seen as weak. In fact, allowing myself to be vulnerable enabled me to connect with the divine soul in front of me as my teacher. That soul could then reflect back to me what I needed to know in order to move along in my next step of evolution. At the same time, that soul could learn his or herown lessons.

Spirit at work unfolded before me and showed me a better way of doing business where love and compassion were paramount. I learned, perhaps for the first time, that abundance resulted when I was in spiritual alignment. My studies were now being integrated into my life, into the real world in which we all live.

You can see what could happen in your own life if every interaction you have goes like this. Imagine what your life would be like!

"Whether outwardly or inwardly, whether in space or time, the farther we penetrate the unknown, the vaster and more marvelous it becomes."

~ *Charles A. Lindbergh,*
Autobiography of Values

Chapter 4

Incomplete Cycles of Action

Think of an incomplete cycle of action as something you started but didn't finish, and now it is weighing on you. It's what pops into your mind and reminds you that you still have unfinished work to do.

Remember the rock-filled backpack you imagined earlier? Each incomplete cycle is like a rock in your backpack. It weighs you down. No single one can bring you to a halt, but collectively, all the weight can slow you down and may prevent you from reaching your goals. Carrying a backpack full of all those rocks makes your back hurt. You are always aware the backpack is there, and it's distracting you from taking in all the beauty around you. You are never free of it, and it always bumps into things. If you could only get rid of all the rocks in your backpack, you would feel lighter, more agile, and better able to move with ease and grace.

Nobody—and I mean *nobody*—would be able to keep up with you if you could clear all those rocks out.

Do you remember the times as a child when you could run easily without any kind of backpack or rocks slowing you down? You could jump and roll on the ground and fit through that hole in the fence and hide under the bed when you were playing with your friends. What you would do to get rid of all these rocks! Where did they all come from?

Are you willing to do what it takes to clear these cycles/rocks out of your life?

Let me tell you about the process I used to get rid of some of mine—about how I cleared an incomplete cycle of action. As I mentioned, I was involved at one time in computer hair imaging. We'd take a video of a person, then superimpose onto their video image twelve to twenty-four different styles and colors of hair. Blondes became redheads and bald men miraculously appeared with dreadlocks. People loved laughing at themselves and their friends, but few people did it more than once. After a few years, the business slowed down, we were on the back side of the cash-flow curve, and my partner and I were both tired of the "video transformation" business. We just wanted to move on.

We had to define how "moving on" was going to look. The business had generated three major assets: A house from which the business operated, a Cessna 182 that was worth no more than what we owed on it, and the business itself.

I had a pretty easy solution for the Cessna 182. The plane was having engine fires and costing huge amounts of money every few months just to keep it running. I simply gave my share of the plane to my partner to make the cash-flow issue go away.

The house and the business weren't quite as easy. It was pretty clear where the dividing line would be drawn on the house and business, and I was willing to fight it out for the house. At the time, which was before the start of my spiritual journey, I was negotiating win/lose deals—and I was never the one on the losing end. This negotiation with my partner was no exception. After a solid month of intense yelling, accusations, hurt feelings, and fighting, my partner reluctantly took the business and gave me the house. I had worn her down, and she no longer wanted to fight. It was causing intense stress and crushing her spirit. It was easier for her to just let it go.

I had declared a Pyrrhic victory once again. My pattern of negotiating win/lose deals had been in full force, and I felt good about it. She had been my dearest friend and greatest supporter, yet I had little concern over the impact of what I had done to her.

Sure enough, everything went well for a time.

About eight years later, I reflected on how I had gotten the better end of that deal. My partner had shut the business down years prior, yet the value of the house had appreciated. I had positive cash flow and was making a profit. All was good on my end.

But Spirit kept sending me reminders of what had happened. Thoughts about the business breakup popped into my mind in the middle of the night while I was trying to sleep and at other random times—such as when I was out with a friend spending some of the money I had made on the house, when I was on vacation, or when someone mentioned my former partner's name. It wasn't going away. I was judging myself as dishonest, mean, cruel, unethical, deceitful, dirty, cold, uncaring, and unappreciative—an overall bad person. Spirit had made this issue one I could no longer ignore, and I didn't want it to take up any more of my time or energy. I decided to call my former partner and apologize.

She was more spiritually evolved than I, and in a calm tone said she had forgiven me years ago. She told me it was something she "had to do." For a time, I hoped her forgiveness might clear this issue for me. But somehow something still didn't seem right. Was my apology too little, too late? Had the damage been done? Was I powerless to undo the damage? I was confused.

A week or two later, I was still thinking about the incident—only now I was thinking about it almost every minute of every day. I realized I hadn't really cleared the issue; I would have to do more to balance things out. I calculated what Susan would have earned if we had sold the property at the time we'd ended the video-business partnership. It amounted to $50,000. I contacted Susan and offered to start paying her that money at 8 percent interest. She became one of my valued investors—complete with title insurance and a lien—and was named as an additional beneficiary on my insurance policy. For the first time in years, I felt good about the situation. I had gone back and cleared this issue. I had dumped a boulder out of my backpack.

I never again woke up thinking about what had happened between Susan and me when the business partnership ended. And it turned out that Spirit was working for both of us: I was helping her out at a time when she needed my help the most, just as she had mentored me in small business at a time when I most needed her help. Things had come full circle. I rebuilt my relationship with her rather than breaking it down. I found the value in connecting with others. My world opened up, and I felt good about helping her. I stopped judging myself, and the crushing weight I'd been carrying lifted almost as soon as I'd hung up the phone. The pain was gone, and I was able to forgive myself for what I had done.

My story had a happy ending, but it was really just the beginning. I've shared this story with several of my friends, and what resulted amazed me. One of them was going through a divorce and was due to receive a $50,000 lump-sum settlement. She asked if I was willing to invest her money. I was shocked that she would even consider investing with me when I had so completely screwed over my former partner years earlier. When I voiced that concern, she explained that anyone who was willing to go back and make things right after eight years was someone she could trust with her money. I was honored by her faith in me; it showed me that I could have a second chance. I don't have to serve a lifetime sentence for making mistakes, and neither do you. None of us is put on the planet perfect—we all have work to do, or we wouldn't be here.

There's even more to the story. My friend's boyfriend had $100,000 to invest—and, equally moved by my story, wanted me to invest his money as well. This money allowed me to buy another property. Since that time he has approached me with an additional $100,000. It seems that once the abundance started to flow, it just kept coming.

Those were just two examples of how I was rewarded for clearing this incomplete cycle of action with Susan. The best was mending the relationship I had with a dear friend and mentor. But there were others. I attracted even more investors. I slept better. And, most important, I was able to remove a really big rock from my backpack. The result was more abundance for me and those investors, who made out with kick-ass investments that paid great dividends for years to come.

"Outer experience is a reflection of inner reality."

~ *Ron and Mary Hulnick*
Loyalty to Your Soul

Chapter 5

You Judge, You Lose

You and I spend countless hours classifying all kinds of things by whether they're good or bad. It's an insidious kind of judging of others and situations that goes on day in and day out. And sadly, our feelings and attitudes get all wrapped up in that judgment.

Here's why: depending on how you classify something, you decide how you feel about it. Has it been a "bad" day? Then you have every right in the world to feel like hell—after all, the Universe dealt you a bad hand. But if something "good" happens—you get approved for a loan or get a promotion—then clearly the gods are smiling on you, and you deserve to celebrate.

Not so fast. You are the one who labels things "good" or "bad"—the Universe doesn't do that.

Maybe it's time to admit that you spend far too much energy classifying the parts of your life into good and bad. Because the way in which you've judged something

may not be accurate at all—or, in many cases, it can change with astonishing speed. This makes judging an unproductive game and a big time-waster.

Let's look at an example:

I rented one of my two-bedroom units to a new tenant who had good credit, did not have pets or kids, and who seemed professional and courteous. I was extremely happy to find her, and I judged the situation as "good."

A few months later, my tenant's boyfriend moved in on the sly. Having two people in the unit instead of one was putting more wear and tear on it. My "good" situation had now become a "bad" one.

The very day I found out the boyfriend had moved into the unit, I found a clause in the lease that allowed me to charge my tenant another $100 for the extra person. That made the situation "good" again. My judgment of things was flipping so fast I could scarcely keep up.

You can probably guess the outcome. My tenants were furious about the extra $100 I demanded; they didn't think they should have to pay extra since the unit had two bedrooms to begin with. Not only did they move out in a rage, causing me to lose rent and face the expense and hassle of finding new tenants, but they sued me. I worried about it every day for a month, right until I walked into court. My situation was no longer "good"; it was definitely "bad."

Oh, but wait. I won in court, so things were now back to being "good."

Or were they? Even though I won in court, the judge awarded the tenants some fees he thought I had unfairly assessed them. In the virtual snap of a finger, there was a judgment against me on my credit report. As a result, the credit reporting agencies dropped my FICO score by one hundred points, which prevented me from getting a loan. Things had now gone to very, very "bad."

The whole experience had been a tremendous roller coaster of emotion, but it wasn't quite over. I was able to have the last say—kind of. I spent a few thousand dollars to get the judgment removed from my credit report, and my favorable credit score was restored. I guess that would make the experience both "good" and "bad": I got my good credit score back, but it cost me several thousand dollars.

And—wait for it—there is a postscript. By the time all of it had been sorted out and my credit score was restored, interest rates had dropped. So the property I was trying to buy (and for which I needed the good credit score) ended up being less expensive than it would have been had I financed it earlier—before all the drama in court involving the credit agencies. What luck! This was clearly a "good" thing.

So what was it? "Good" or "bad"?

You can easily see from my example that things can be both. Or neither. And that begs the question: *Do we ever really know if things are good or bad?* I'd like to suggest something that may sound radical to you. Lots of things are out of your control. They simply are what they are. And in those cases, maybe you'd be better off to suspend judgment. You can save yourself a lot of emotional ups and downs and a whole lot of energy if you just decide to trust that everything happens for our betterment. One way or another.

Then there are things that are at least partially in your control. Look again at my experience with my tenants. Some parts of that situation (the ways in which I responded) were in my control, and some things (the ways in which my tenants responded) were not something I could control. By assigning a label of "good" or "bad" on the things that happened, I effectively eliminated my ability to respond in better ways. Think of all the time, frustration, and expense I could have saved if I had tapped into Spirit and reached some sort of settlement with these tenants without going to court? I wouldn't have lost them as tenants. I wouldn't have incurred the costs of renovating the unit, running ads, answering calls, and interviewing new tenants—not to mention the substantial cost of repairing my credit score and the rent I lost in the meantime.

What it all comes down to is this: Judging circumstances as good or bad, judging other people, and judging yourself, usually makes situations worse and prolongs suffering.

To take this a step further, it's impossible to judge someone else without judging yourself as well. If I judge someone as a bad tenant, I consequently judge myself as a bad landlord because I'm the one who chose the tenant. If I judge my workers as incompetent,

I am judging myself as the bad boss who hired them or failed to train them well enough. It's a vicious cycle of finger-pointing that inevitably points back at you, so why even do it? The time it takes to throw this energy around could be spent so much more productively.

If judgment is so clearly negative, you may wonder why you do it. The answer is simple: you and I, all of us, have a very difficult time seeing this behavior in ourselves. The person you judge becomes a mirror so you can see yourself, and that's a harrowing concept. No one wants to be as wrong as the person he or she is judging.

I saw a great example of this on a hike with one of my friends. She complained that her boyfriend was not being honest regarding his ex-wife and children. As he frantically tried to keep his web of lies together, he was becoming more and more entangled. My friend had been dealing with this for longer than a year, and she was becoming increasingly upset.

"You've attracted him as a mirror," I explained. Maybe if you look at how you're being dishonest—"

She cut me off in a fit of rage and yelled, "How can you say that? I'm not a liar!"

"You are lying to yourself by thinking things are going to change," I told her.

My friend stopped on the trail, totally dumbfounded.

It's happened to me, and I'm confident it has happened to you. When God orchestrates something like this to teach us to love ourselves and others—free of judgment—valuable lessons are learned on both sides.

"The universe presents us with endless opportunities to synchronize our path with our truth."
~ *Jeff Brown*

Chapter 6

Integrity

Are you in integrity in your business? Are you in integrity in your life? Are there things that have transpired that you could have done better? Have you burned a bridge or two along the way? Are there things that you have said or done that just don't feel right? (Maybe these are the things you do when nobody is looking or that nobody will ever know about.) Would you sleep better at night if you were able to clear some of these things up? Would you feel lighter?

Once I started really thinking about integrity, I realized that my way of doing business needed to change. One example involved the way in which my company was reporting expenses. My handyman provided us with cash receipts for the materials he bought to make repairs to the properties; we in turn used those receipts for a tax deduction. I suddenly realized that the handyman also was billing us for labor and materials—and the materials were being deducted as an expense by our accountant, who didn't realize that these materials were the same ones that had already been itemized on the cash receipts. In other words, the materials were being deducted twice.

When I recognized what was happening, I could have just let it slide since we had plenty of documentation to support our position. Instead, I set up a credit card account at Home Depot for all materials we used, which eliminated all cash purchases.

My company was now operating in integrity. But that wasn't the only benefit: I accumulated frequent flyer miles on my credit card that were honestly earned and that were a bonus for me. On one business trip, I used 750,000 frequent flyer miles to fly two guests and myself to Africa, and then two of us went on to the Seychelles for a second vacation.

Another example involved a contract I had for a set of coin-operated washers and dryers on a property I had just purchased. In the past, I would have broken the contract by just disconnecting the machines and setting them aside. I would have sent the coin-op company a very nasty letter in legal-sounding language telling them to come and pick up the machines because they were in my way and were preventing me from generating income. I would have threatened a lawsuit if they didn't act quickly. This bully-like way of doing business had always worked for me in the past, but it required a huge amount of energy involving lots of screaming and intensity. When I conducted myself like that, I knew I was out of integrity, and I was making a lot of enemies along the way.

To break this cycle—and to relieve myself of the stress—I decided to act with integrity instead of falling into my usual pattern of behavior. I decided to meet with the coin-op company representative. But first I needed a plan. I was unsure of what to do, so I sat in silence on a regular basis until one day I came up with a solution.

I had two other properties in rough parts of town where the machines were frequently broken into and the coins stolen. Since I had to repair and sometimes replace the machines, I netted zero income. I proposed that the coin-op company remove their machines from the property I had just purchased and install card-activated machines at the other locations so we could test out our new business relationship. I promised that if the arrangement worked for both of us, we would install card-activated machines at the newer properties. I'd found a win/win solution, and I'd maintained my integrity. The energy drain finally came to an end.

The energy drain wasn't the only thing that stopped. I found that by operating with integrity, I also quieted the voice inside my head that had repeatedly told me, "You are not honest," "You are a cheater," "You don't respect yourself enough to do what is right," "You can't be trusted," and "People won't like you if they find out who you are and what you are doing." As you can imagine, hearing that "voice" was like engaging in a gang fight every day—with *myself*.

If you're not behaving with integrity, you've got a similar "voice" in your head that will be only too happy to tell you about it. If you haven't heard it, find a place free of distraction and carefully listen. The voice—Spirit—is always talking; you just have to listen. Spirit brings to your conscious mind what you need to work on when you have the bandwidth to deal with it. In fact, Spirit will keep repeating it if you miss it the first, second, or third time.

I like to think of these experiences with Spirit like holding a beach ball under water. It's easy to hold the ball under the water for a while, and the surface of the water even appears to be calm. But it takes a *lot* of energy to keep that inflated ball under the water for very long—just as it takes a huge amount of energy to maintain the illusion when you actually need to change the way you behave. As you push against that ball with all your might, sooner or later your arms will give way and the ball will rocket to the surface for everyone to see. And that's exactly how Spirit works.

As an indication of divine involvement in our lives, Spirit comes back stronger and stronger each time with the lessons we need to learn. It's not some sort of cosmic torture; instead, Spirit will stick with you as long as it takes for you to learn and start applying the lessons, because the lessons we need to learn are so important for us to survive and thrive. Just like the beach ball whose pressure drives it to the surface of the water, the lessons will eventually become so powerful that you can't ignore them any longer. The beach ball will explode to the surface, and so will the lessons. So why not learn sooner rather than later? Attend to and learn the lessons on the first pass so you can clear them and operate in an attitude of joy until the next series of lessons is presented. It's like studying hard so you can pass a test in school the first time instead of having to spend time in study hall during recess and after school so you can take the test again. If you flunk enough tests, you'll never see recess again and you'll have to repeat the entire year.

You can't avoid the lessons you need to learn, so you might as well deal with them now—and integrity is a big one. Consider this: you are being given an opportunity to dramatically improve your life. A lack of integrity is like a leaky pipe under the kitchen sink. If you continue to ignore it, the damage will eventually become extreme; the wood under the sink may even rot away. But if you call the plumber at the first sign of trouble—in other words, if you make the effort right now to change your way of doing things—it may cost you a bit, but things aren't going to get any worse. They will only get better, and you will enjoy years of abundance and peace.

"Our deepest fear is not that we are inadequate. Our deepest fear is that we are powerful beyond measure."

~Marianne Williamson

Chapter 7

Gratitude

People used to tell me all the time that I needed to express gratitude. But I was baffled. How was I supposed to express gratitude when I hadn't yet changed my life and business enough to be thankful? It seemed like trying to put the cart before the horse.

But I was wrong. Actually, the exact opposite is true.

Let me give you a great example of the difference gratitude can make, even when your *perception* is all that has changed. For the past ten years, I've walked through Balboa Park in San Diego almost every day. The park has museums, a beautiful bridge, ponds, restaurants, statues, amphitheaters, flowers, fountains, a variety of fish, birds, and much more. The energy there is wonderful. It revitalizes and uplifts me. It helps me renew the connection I have with the planet and other living things.

One day about five years ago, as I was walking in the park, I was feeling immense amounts of gratitude in my

life. I felt happy to be alive. I counted all my blessings, and life seemed to be going well. I sensed that I was unconditionally loved and that Spirit loved me so fully it was as if all my experiences existed for my growth and evolution. It seemed Spirit was embracing me.

With that sudden awareness, I began to notice that the grass appeared greener than it ever had before. It was even greener than I thought possible. The birds were chirping the most delightful songs, as if they were thanking God for their very existence; the sky was the deepest blue, and the billowing clouds reflected the sunlight. The air was perfectly cool, fresh, and crisp. I had never before experienced the park at that level. Nothing at all had changed in the park since my walk the day before; what had changed was my *perception*. What had changed was my ability to see the park through the lens of *gratitude*. Today I refer to these walks as my "gratitude walks."

That change extended far beyond the park. It was like I'd been given the "Life 2.0" version of things, divinely inspired by God. It was like someone had turned the intensity knob on life all the way up. Each successive click changed my perception of the world around me. I was waking up as though opening my eyes to life for the first time, overwhelmed by what I was seeing. My sense of reality changed instantly and forever. I was euphoric, and I never wanted it to end. Life had become a living prayer.

I wondered what life would be like if I felt that level of gratitude every day. I wondered if I could have that experience in my relationships with my family, my friends, and in my romantic relationship. It was incredible to consider what was possible if I could have that intensity in my business life. I imagined what that would look like and where it could take my business. It occurred to me that I could work fewer hours, have more time for vacations, argue less with others, go to court less often. It would very likely mean greater abundance, better cash flow, and more properties—manifested as a result of cocreating, not goal feasting. I believed life would be much less overwhelming. In fact, I realized I had just stumbled onto a concept that could change my entire life.

If you're not used to experiencing or expressing gratitude, you may not think you have things for which you can be thankful. But you do, and the sooner you recognize that, the greater your experience will be. Think about your family. Your health. The air you breathe. The water you drink. The beauty that surrounds you in the world (just like I discovered the beauty in the park). The fact that your body can heal itself when it's injured. How about being grateful for *you*? *You are a magnificent, divine creature. As you learn to experience and express gratitude, you'll find that it's a magical mindset from which to operate.* If I'm not having critical thoughts but instead feeling gratitude, isn't that a better use of my time?

The greatest demonstration of gratitude I have ever experienced came on a flying trip in South Africa. I was headed to the Kliptown Youth Facility, which was

located in a slum in Soweto, South Africa. As we approached, I started having flashbacks to a two-and-a-half-year period of my childhood when I lived in Jakarta, Indonesia. I remember seeing total poverty in Indonesia; there were people who lived in shacks made of cardboard, tin sheets, discarded wood, and other materials scavenged at the dump. The poor often placed their huts next to the water so they could wash, brush their teeth, and use the water as a toilet. As a child growing up in Indonesia, I made a judgment about those people and their conditions, perceiving the situation as dirty and gross.

I could feel something happening inside of me as we got closer to the Kliptown Youth Facility. My stomach churned, and the pressure building in my head made me feel as if I was going to explode. Rationally, though, I knew that my experience was going to be different than it had been in Indonesia. Thanks to my graduate studies in spiritual psychology, I was in a different place in my evolution.

When we arrived, we were warmly greeted by the staff and immediately given a tour of the facility. I noticed how tightly packed the people were in their little shacks. The facility smelled of sweat and body waste; stray dogs ran everywhere, and filthy water flowed down the dirt streets. When our group eventually reached the kitchen, I asked if I could help in any way. Someone handed me a bag of oranges and asked me to give each child in the food line an orange. I quickly realized that the oranges must have been genetically modified—they were closer to the size of large grapefruit.

The first children in line were three small boys ages ten, eight, and six. As I reached out to give an orange to the first child, he put his hands together in front of his face, bowed his head in appreciation, and looked into my eyes with an expression of immense gratitude unlike any I had ever before seen. It was if he was looking through me and connecting with my soul.

As I handed him the orange, I got tunnel vision directly to his face. It was as if I were seeing him being magnified in four successive stages until all I could see was his face. I was seeing a child express more gratitude for a simple orange than I had ever expressed for anything in my entire life. Then the most remarkable thing happened: in an instant his face went from that of a ten-year-old boy to that of an eighty-year-old man. I rocked back on my heels in shock, gasping for air; I wondered if I might be losing my mind. I looked around, but no one seemed to see what was happening.

As I handed an orange to the next boy in line, the eight-year-old, the same thing happened again—my tunnel vision, his instant aging, his expression of deep, intense gratitude. It was as though his entire earthly being—from child- to adulthood—was thanking me for that simple orange.

Finally, I turned to the third boy, who was about six years old, and had the exact experience a third time. But the experience was the most dramatic this third time, perhaps because the boy was the youngest. By

this time I was dizzy and confused, unsure of what was going to happen next. I was scared. I wondered if I was dreaming, but at the same time wondered how I would ever possibly explain what had happened in my dream. I was experiencing a lesson of gratitude so powerful I knew I'd never be the same, now that I knew what was possible.

I later learned that what I'd witnessed in slums of Soweto is called transmutation. We are actually living all the stages of our lives at once, since time is just a human concept. Through transmutation, some have the ability to travel between the various stages of life as though living them simultaneously. That night I woke up sobbing, feeling such compassion for the people I had met that day. I had learned one of the most valuable lessons of my life. Spirit helped me to put into words what I believe I experienced:

Have you ever had one of those instances where you stop breathing, and as you shake you realize that you are experiencing a moment you will never forget? Where your eyes lock with someone who has taught you something on a level deeper than you ever imagined possible? And where you realize in that moment that you have just been woven into the tapestry of life, pulled a bit deeper into "gratitude" and "oneness" than you believed or knew was possible? Where this perceived stranger grabs hold of your heart and tugs so hard on your soul that he reminds you that your purpose was never anything but simply to love as deeply and completely as you can with all your heart?

There are moments that take our breath away, like when we are surprised by a thoughtful person's selfless act of kindness. And then there are moments, though rare, when time just stops—like when we spot our lifetime mate for the first time, or when we see a glimpse of our life's purpose here on the planet, or when we connect with each other on a level much deeper than we ever imagined possible. It is during these moments that we finally see the connection between all of us; we realize we are simply one. These are the moments where you realize the shared tears, experiences, and journey indicate that this honor is not about one person but about all of us and what we have accomplished together—what is possible only through this magical connection that is love.

The deep sort of gratitude I witnessed and experienced is something you can experience as well. And it can influence your state of mind throughout each and every day of your life. When you see the world around you through the lens of gratitude, it's what you take with you into every transaction, interaction, and conversation. The people you deal with will recognize it, feel it, and respond to it. It will become your calling card. It is what is meant by the word Namaste, which means "The Spirit within me salutes the Spirit in you."

You have been given the opportunity to live in any state of mind you choose. If you select gratitude as your primary way of being, you can approach each situation with a mindset of love and compassion rather than anger or upset. Imagine how people will respond

to you when you approach them with this kind of gratitude. It's easy. Think about how you would feel if someone approached you in that same way—as if he were blessed to see you and thrilled to do business with you. Think what a difference that would make to every transaction you enter.

You can choose a better life for yourself. So much more is possible when you use the help that Spirit makes available to you—and keep in mind that it is available without limitation, free of charge, and is the best help available on the planet. All you have to do is know it when you see it. Just as when you meet someone special, you can recognize God in your life.

My experiences in the park and in South Africa are just a few of the events that have made me very aware of the importance of expressing gratitude daily and before I go to sleep each night. What a perfect state of mind to be in before I reconnect with Spirit. Try it yourself and you will realize how divinely blessed you are to be given so many opportunities to live and love.

"All journeys have secret destinations of which the traveler is unaware."

~ *Martin Buber*

Chapter 8

Timing: Let It Go

Timing is so critical—in both business and in life. Timing can be the thing that determines whether a deal actually happens or not. And in many cases, we have no control over timing.

Here's one of the most important things to know: Everything is happening in divine order. When something is delayed, instead of getting frustrated, realize that it could be Spirit orchestrating something even more important and divine in your life.

The next time you feel that your timing is off, for whatever reason—wait. Have faith. Realize that Spirit has a bigger plan for you and that things are unfolding as they have been planned for your greatest good. Sometimes if the timing went according to *your* plan, you might miss out on some valuable lessons.

I've learned this firsthand, and here's a great example: My plan was to fly myself around the world, and during the months I waited to take off on that once-in-a-lifetime opportunity, I needed somewhere to live. I thought I had the timing all worked out, but Spirit apparently had other plans—and take a look at what happened.

I applied to rent a condo in San Diego that would serve as my crash pad while I prepared for my flight around the world. My own units were fully rented—and even if they hadn't been, I didn't own a unit in the exact place I wanted to live. So I went out on the open market, just like anyone else. I submitted my application and didn't have any concerns. I felt my application was very strong based on my credit score, my twenty-two years in business, my monthly income, my assets, and the equity I had on my buildings.

Imagine how surprised I was when my application was denied. Apparently the landlord felt I had too many properties and that any downturn in the economy would result in me going belly up.

I could have slipped into a depressed state over how I hadn't gotten the condo, how life wasn't fair, and how I'd been discriminated against because I had too many buildings. Instead, I laughed at lunacy of the situation. In a situation like this, you can learn a lot from a toddler: when a toddler falls down, he doesn't judge himself as wrong or stupid for falling. Instead, he sees his fall as part of the process of learning to walk. He just gets up, dusts himself off, and makes another attempt at walking. And that's pretty much what I did. I got up, dusted myself off, and made another attempt at this adventure called life.

I talked to the agent who had helped me find the condo, and he pointed out the obvious: telling the owner about all my properties didn't help me. Valuable lesson #1. I didn't want to relive the first experience, so I decided to write a letter to any new landlord explaining why I was the best candidate for the property.

In my letter, I spelled out in plain terms why having a bunch of properties was not "bad"—I had equity, positive cash flow, and low levels of vacancy. I explained that it actually gave me a buffer in the event of a downturn in the economy. I figured that some additional communication was just the thing to make the transaction happen this time.

Valuable lesson #2: The process of writing that letter, of having to "defend" myself and my position, made me think (for the first time) of how challenging it must be for a new tenant to rent in today's market. Maybe Spirit was giving me an opportunity to look at the process I was using to rent to new tenants—or to see with clarity how others must feel when they tried to rent from me. Maybe Spirit was even giving me the chance to see what a difficult job my rental agent was having trying to rent to new tenants. I saw the need for some important changes in my process—something I never would have realized had *my* timing worked out on the San Diego condo.

As luck would have it, the person who was first awarded the condo didn't have the credit he had claimed, so I did eventually get the unit.

But the lessons didn't stop at this point. It seemed that the Universe still wanted to teach me valuable lesson #3: I needed to learn empathy, and Spirit had just the plan.

Just a week after I had settled into the condo in San Diego and flown to Colorado to visit some friends, the unit above my condo caught fire; the sprinkler system went off and completely flooded the unit. And that's not all: hundreds of gallons of water flowed through the walls of my unit as well as the three below it. The next few weeks were a major challenge as I tried to work around the damage and manage the repairs in my unit.

And here's the amazing thing: at this same time I experienced a dramatic rise in the number of tenant complaints about lack of follow-up on repair requests. The misery I was experiencing as I dealt with the damages to my condo in San Diego was clearly arranged to let me know what my tenants were dealing with at the same time. You can imagine I was much more responsive to their complaints and requests than I had ever been before.

Now I was ready for my lesson on empathy. I was always furious when tenants asked for what I perceived to be out-of-line requests. But there in Colorado I found myself negotiating with my new San Diego landlord for a free month of rent in exchange for all the inconvenience I was experiencing as a result of the flooded unit. I received what I asked for. And I went forward realizing that my tenants weren't out to manipulate or use me. It was suddenly much easier for me to see things from their point of view.

I had learned four valuable lessons that are making a significant difference in my business and in my life. I owe it all to the timing Spirit had in mind. Look what I might have missed out on learning had my application been approved and had I moved effortlessly into the condo in San Diego.

As you think about this, please remember one important thing: you never know when a particular lesson will be the last one. Lessons are a lot like onions; some are large, and it takes time to peel away the individual layers. Others are like small cocktail onions that can be dispatched in a single bite.

Remember, too, that there's always a final exam. When Spirit teaches a valuable lesson, the final exam makes sure you've learned exactly what you're supposed to learn. And it's not an easy exam. While it can be extremely challenging, you're getting it not because Spirit is looking to torture you but because you are loved so much. If Spirit didn't care, all this energy would not be put into organizing a series of events perfectly synchronized into a lesson plan for your highest good.

Oh, and one more thing: We all experience upset. When timing gets thrown off and something really crummy happens, sometimes our response is to "lose it." I've lost it before, and I'm pretty sure you have too. Don't beat yourself up when it happens, but don't wallow in it, either. Do whatever it takes to quickly move back into a place of gratitude and balance. The longer you stay in a place of upset, the less time you have to bask in gratitude and experience the love that serves you and those around you in the most divine way.

"My soul is in the sky."

~ William Shakespeare

Chapter 9

Listen

One of the most fundamental skills you can bring to the business table is the ability to communicate effectively. It seems so simple, but I have found that most of us have never been trained to communicate effectively—not in school, not by family, and certainly not in business.

Key to effective communication is the ability to listen, and I needed to learn how to actually listen to people. Before, I was so focused on trying to anticipate what the other person was going to say or on formulating a response that I totally missed what they were trying to say. I used to interrupt others with defensive comments, and often my attempts at communication would drive me further from the other person than when we started. I often missed an opportunity to resolve an issue because the other person just wanted to be heard and I wouldn't listen. Maybe you're in a similar spot.

Here's a simple first step: repeat what you heard the other person say in your own words; it's a way to perception check and make sure you heard correctly. Start with a statement like, "What I heard you say was…" The other person now knows he or she has been heard and will be more likely to listen to you as well. You will connect with others instead of moving apart from one another.

I recall once receiving a letter from a tenant who was very dissatisfied with my company. The letter was so acerbic that my bookkeeper handed it to me at arm's length by its very edge, like she would a dirty sock.

It took me three attempts to read the letter because it was so hateful and angry. I kept getting a sick feeling in my stomach. The tenant called me a slumlord and accused my entire staff of incompetence. The tenant's toilet had clogged and overflowed. In the multiple attempts that were made to clear the main line, his bedroom and living room had been flooded with sewage from the other units. This "shit storm" soaked the carpets, and walking across them now created a squishing sound, like someone stepping on a dirty sponge. In fact, when the handyman removed the toilet, the sewage from the other units splashed all over the walls in an explosive plume of waste.

I made several calls to those involved to find out if things were as bad as the letter described. I anticipated some exaggerations and miscommunications; in this case there were a few, but the situation was truly dreadful!

I contacted the tenant to tell him how sorry I was that this had happened and to let him know we would resolve the issue quickly. I told him what I had learned from my calls and wanted to repeat back what I understood had happened to him. *I wanted him to know he had been heard.* I asked him if I had gotten it right. He added some additional details. I listened carefully, and then *I repeated back what he had told me.*

I described my plan for making the situation right. I told him we would clean the subfloor and replace the carpet and pad. I gave him a rent concession and paid him for the time he'd spent cleaning the sewage off the walls in the bathroom, acknowledging that his time had value. Finally, I let him know that the condo I had just rented had flooded out and that, like him, I was dealing with some challenges. I told him I understood what he was going through. I had walked a mile in his shoes that were wet with sewage.

In that moment, I wondered if my experience with the flooding had occurred so I could be empathetic to my tenant's experience. We were learning together. Our experience was divine and meant to happen so we could both have more compassion.

My tenant later apologized for the harshness of his letter. He followed up the next day with an e-mail, apologizing again and thanking us for all we had done.

The key take-away from this story is the importance of listening. Genuinely listen. Repeat back what you hear. Express compassion. Then take the appropriate action with integrity.

The letter I received from that tenant was probably the harshest one I've ever received. But the way I reacted turned what seemed to be a toxic situation into an opportunity to connect with my tenant, and it took only a few minutes. I avoided a lawsuit and kept a good tenant. In fact, that same tenant went on to become a supporter of my company and efforts in the future. You have the same power to transform almost any situation; you just need to use your new tools.

Perhaps the bigger lesson is that you can communicate much more effectively when you realize we are all mirrors of each other. We ultimately connect because all of us are made from the same stuff; all of us experience the same feelings; all of us are part of this thriving living planet. We all have the same purpose: to love each other unconditionally in the most challenging of times, which is when we need it the very most.

"The reason birds can fly and we can't is simply that they have perfect faith, for to have faith is to have wings."

~ *Sir James Matthew Barrie*

Chapter 10

Direct Communication with Spirit

Being able to communicate with others is key to your success—but that's not the only kind of communication you need to master. Ask yourself this: How often do I directly talk to God/Spirit? Are you afraid to ask for what you truly want or need? Do you even know how to ask? You have this divine source of help available twenty-four hours a day, seven days a week. Maybe it's time you make use of the help that's available.

I had just finished my third year of advanced graduate work in spiritual psychology, and it was as if my entire life was pumped. I felt so much gratitude for all the things my spiritual studies had brought about in the previous few years. My business had tripled. That enabled me to achieve my dream of buying a plane, and as a result of that I had flown myself to thirty countries in three years. The experience of flying all over the world had led to great spiritual growth and awareness.

In a quiet moment one day, I decided that it would be fun to lecture on the topics of *spirituality* and *business*, and *spirituality in aviation*, which are my passions. I said to Spirit, "If you want me to spend the next one to two years giving back by lecturing and by writing articles, blogs, and books on these topics, I need three things from you so I can free up my time:

1) My house that I've been trying to sell for three-and-a-half years and that is currently rented to tenants needs to sell.
2) All my vacant units need to be rented.
3) My twenty-eight-unit building that just burned, causing the sprinkler system to dump five thousand gallons of water in five minutes, needs to become a nonissue. (More on this story in Chapter 12). The more I thought about lecturing, the scarier it sounded to me, and so I figured I had just made it virtually impossible for Spirit to meet my requirements. After all, I'd been trying unsuccessfully to sell my house for three and a half years, and I'd done *everything* I could think to do—including burying a statue of St. Anthony upside down in the backyard.

Turns out I didn't need to second-guess Spirit. Within two weeks, I had an all-cash offer on my house that was due to close in a week, the insurance company was offering me three times the damages I had incurred on the twenty-eight-unit building in addition to $170,000 in lost rent money, and all my vacant units had been rented. Period.

I had never received a clearer message from Spirit. I could easily dismiss one of these things as sheer luck. But *two* of them? And there's no way all three could have happened at the same time, right after I requested them, without Spirit operating in my life.

You don't always have to have the answer. Spirit can do the heavy lifting for you. You just have to ask Spirit directly and allow things to unfold. And realize this: the things you ask Spirit for are more likely to happen if they better the lives of others, move the planet ahead, and bring you closer to others.

My experience is a perfect example of how the things I asked were in perfect alignment and for the greater good of all involved. The funds generated from these efforts would pay for the costs of getting the word out. Spirit again showed me that the more I gave, the more I would receive—not just in reimbursement for my efforts, but also in valuable life lessons that I could apply every day to bring my life into spiritual growth and alignment.

“The engine is the heart of an airplane,
but the pilot is its soul.”

~Walter Raleigh

Chapter 11

Listening in the Silence

My favorite spiritual practice is one called "listening in the silence." Author and energy healing expert Caroline Myss got it right when she said, "Silence is the oxygen of the soul."

Silence allows you to connect with your inner self. It brings about a situation of calm. You are no longer over stimulated by all the chatter, distractions, and noise that occurs in your daily life. Silence provides a time to connect with Spirit and the collective consciousness, which is where you find all the information you need available to you.

As a pilot, I've experienced the joy of countless hours of being in silence. During my solo flight across the North Atlantic and polar ice cap to Europe, as well as during my flight across the Bering Sea to Siberia, I sat quietly for more than eighty hours. During those silent hours I found myself thinking, receiving, and appreciating life as I looked out over some of the most beautiful parts of the planet I had ever seen. Because of what I was able to experience during that profound silence, these were by far the most profound and revelatory journeys of my life.

When silence surrounds you, you are able to connect with your intuition and receive downloads from the divine. During these moments of clarity is when Spirit talks to us directly. You might think of them in the popular vernacular of "aha" moments, the times when you realize you have the right answer to the question you asked.

Perhaps most importantly, silence provides an opportunity to ask Spirit direct questions. You'll have your own questions, determined by the things that are of pressing importance to you. Some questions I like to ask are, "What I can to do be of greatest service?" "I am totally overwhelmed with this situation; what is my next step?" "I accept whatever lesson you have for me; will you help me learn it with ease and grace?" Sometimes I simply utter, "Thy will be done."

I recall a situation in which I felt my world was falling apart in the most dramatic fashion. I was overwhelmed by three things that were happening at the same time. In the first, I was defending myself in court against two separate tenant lawsuits claiming I had not returned enough of their deposits. In the second, my mom's best friend had just died, bringing up unresolved issues I had related to my mother's death. And in the third—as if things weren't already bad enough—my girlfriend had found another guy to date; he was a doctor (like her), her spiritual mentor, and a twin-engine pilot (which added insult to injury!).

As I walked through the metal detector at the courthouse and got the "beep," indicating that I was okay to continue, I could barely breathe. I was having a full-blown anxiety attack, feeling short of breath and totally overloaded and unable to tell which way was up. I was not ready to give my best performance in court while under what I perceived was a cosmic barrage of lessons to learn.

I walked around outside the courthouse for a few minutes before my case was scheduled to begin and was able to find a little space apart from other people. Walking has always been a peaceful experience for me, taking me back to many happy times in Balboa Park. When I walk, my breathing becomes more regular, I start to notice the beautiful things in my world, and time slows down. As I walked around outside the courthouse, I got a download that I was going to be okay—that I needed to handle things one at time. I would be fine. I recognized that all three of these situations were learning experiences for my personal growth, and they were being brought to the surface so I could heal them. I was loved unconditionally, regardless of anything I had gotten myself into.

Many of the great masters—including Leonardo Da Vinci, Albert Einstein, and Michelangelo—walked in nature as a daily practice to get clarity on things they did not understand. As they walked, they expressed

gratitude and reflected on the burning questions in their minds. They connected with the earth and saw the beauty before them. They experienced "oneness" with all of creation and recognized that we are all connected.

Life often presents you with what seems the impossible task of figuring things out given a limitless number of variables. You could spend all day trying to calculate the solutions. Instead, simply be open to what Spirit has for you. Spend your time in silent thought and focused energy, looking not for the ultimate solutions but for the next step as it unfolds in front of you. Doing so lifts an enormous burden, allowing you to move through life with grace and ease.

Many times over the course of writing this book, I've taken a break, gone on a walk through the meadow at Squaw Valley, and simply asked Spirit for guidance. If I didn't have an example for a particular chapter, didn't know how to finish things off, or needed more content, I asked to be a channel for what Spirit wanted me to share. Each time, the answer either popped into my mind or a conversation with someone revealed exactly what I needed to know. The Bible says, "Ask and ye shall receive." I believe that to be true.

When you surround yourself with silence, you get something that is called *perspective*, or *altitude*. You become elevated to a point where you can see everything. I've had that experience as a pilot: as I gain altitude, I can see so much more at twenty-five thousand feet than I can at one thousand. Lakes, rivers, mountains, and other airports come into view; the picture is more complete, and I can see how things relate to each other. It's all about perspective: I can see how rivers feed the lakes. I can see how the Southern California coastal moisture dumps on the west side of the mountains, making them lush and green, in contrast to the dry east side. With altitude and perspective, I can understand why there are deserts for hundreds of miles to the east and why the coastal fog often burns off as it reaches the land.

Let's go back to the three overwhelming situations that were causing me so much stress and look at them from a thirty-thousand-foot perspective. Let's see what that altitude and perspective, provided by Spirit, helped me learn.

In response to the first situation, I realized that the legal system was not the solution to my problem. I realized that there had to be a better way of doing business than going to court every few months. I changed my way of doing business. I started screening prospective tenants more thoroughly on the front end. I began doing full credit checks on the people applying for tenancy. I called their references. And I started having a detailed conversation with the people that I rented to, establishing a relationship of trust.

My response to the second situation wasn't as easy or straightforward; I had a lot of work to do. I needed to forgive my mother for dying so unexpectedly, and I needed to forgive myself for the irrational thought that she had died intentionally. I realized that Mom did the very best she could and loved me unconditionally. Her passing taught me that each instant is to be valued. There were other things I was eventually able to resolve as well. The important thing isn't what I *did*, it was that I was inspired to seek answers in an attempt to solve the unhealed situation.

And the third situation, which involved my girlfriend, taught me that, ultimately, we wanted different things in life. I needed to find a way to work past conflict rather than just give up on people when relationship issues arose. I needed to accept that someone else's fears and emotions were real and valid to them, even if they seemed irrational to me.

The most important thing that came out of these three situations was my understanding that Spirit did not present me with these challenges to hurt me, punish me, or slow me down, but rather so that I could heal them, learn from them, and move forward. I have found that when I learn these lessons quickly, my life opens up and I benefit from what I have learned right away. And I have noted that after the lessons are learned, I experience an extended period of time where life is blissful, even euphoric. You will find the same thing in your life. I believe this is our reward for our lessons learned.

Please know that Spirit doesn't always give you exactly what you ask for. Spirit knows what you need much better than you do. At the conclusion of any request of Spirit, I like to say, "Please give me this or something better for the highest good of all concerned."

If you ask Spirit to make you a better painter, you may be provided with a canvas, paint, other supplies, and the opportunity to learn painting skills. Similarly, if you ask Spirit to grant you courage, you may be given a war of your own where you can learn to be brave and courageous under fire. Keep your eyes and your heart open to what Spirit gives you so you can use all of it to achieve the thing for which you asked.

I once asked Spirit for a plane so I could realize my childhood fantasy of flying. Instead, Spirit gave me a set of spiritual principles and practices. I didn't wake up one day to find a plane in my front yard. But I was able to use the spiritual principles and practices I was given to triple my business. With the income from that business growth, my plane became a reality.

The lesson didn't stop there. Flying has played a huge role in my spiritual development. When I am piloting a plane, I am most aware of my direct connection with Spirit. My experience of gratitude, oneness, and silence is unparalleled. Many of my most significant breakthroughs have come while I have been flying. I have found that flying is my meditation and my gateway to more love, abundance, and connection. My plane is appropriately named Euphoria because it describes the experience of flying her and because she plays a big part in making my aviation lectures, my writing, and my spirituality possible. That, too, is part of the gift Spirit gave me.

"Stop the words now. Open the window in the center of your chest and let the spirits fly in and out."

~ *Rumi*

Chapter 12

Surrender

I know what you're thinking—*Surrender*? If you're like most people, *surrender* has all sorts of negative connotations. It means giving up. Letting go. Losing control. Surrender is scary. And even if you're not scared, you're almost sure to be more than a little uncomfortable at the thought of surrendering.

I want you to put those negative connotations out of your mind. Yes, truly. Of all the concepts I share in this book, surrender may require the greatest leap of faith. But believe me when I say that the answer to your problems may be found by giving up control and letting go. You will be amazed at what happens when you take your hands off the cosmic steering wheel and trust that things will happen as Spirit intends.

And if that's not sobering enough, let's take it a step further: What if you turned everything in your life over to Spirit? What if you had total faith that whatever—and I do mean whatever—you were to experience was going to be handled by Spirit for your highest good? Could you go to bed at night and just simply pray, "Thy will be done?"

Think of how it might feel to trust Spirit with everything. It's actually an incredibly freeing feeling. Spirit will guide you on matters of importance; all you have to do is look for the signs and go with them.

Lots of people are scared to death about the notion of giving up control. But let's get real. Look at your life and take an honest inventory of the things over which you truly have control. You're just like me and everyone else: You will quickly find that you have control over almost nothing. You can't control the weather or the timing of earthquakes, tsunamis, tornados. You can't control the length of days. You can't control the feelings and actions of others. Even if you eat well and exercise and get regular checkups, you can't control the fact that you will eventually die. (As a friend once quipped, "None of us is getting out of here alive; it's just a matter of when.") In fact, you can't control most aspects of your life.

With that in mind, why not just completely and totally surrender? Why waste all that energy fighting what you can't control? When it all comes down to it, what a waste of good time, right?

I have reached the point in my journey where the most amazing things are happening to me. I no longer need to figure things out. I just put my energy into letting things happen. I set an intention each night that if God has more work for me to do, or another lesson for me to learn, I'll accept it. The only thing I ask is that I can learn my lessons with grace and ease.

Don't get me wrong: I know it's not easy at first. In fact, the first time I did it, overwhelming feelings of panic flooded over me. I started sweating, swearing more than usual, and questioning pretty much everything—including God. But after a while, I noticed that life was moving along just fine. Things were *not* out of control at all. In fact, they were going along quite well. I was following my intuition, knowing that what God had in store for me—for all of us—was infinitely better than what I could ever dream for myself.

I was given a wonderful gift during the Christmas holiday of 2014. I woke to a call from my assistant. He told me that my beautiful twenty-eight-unit building had burst into flame early that morning. The sprinklers had gone off as they were supposed to, and I later learned that more than five thousand gallons of water had been sprayed into the building in all of five minutes.

Water and fire are two of the most destructive elements you can introduce into a building. By the grace of God, all the tenants made it out safely; the Red Cross moved them to a temporary shelter, and all were fine for the time being. Between the rapidly growing mold from the water and the smoky odor from the fire, major work would be required to bring the building back to livable condition.

I watched in relative calm as the 5:00, 7:00, and 9:00 evening news detailed how both the fire and sprinkle-

shower had destroyed a large portion of my three-story wood building. A major life event was unfolding right before my eyes, and I was powerless to do anything about it except watch in disbelief. I remember thinking that things like this did happen but wondering why they were happening to me. But because of my trust in Spirit, I knew there was a reason for it that would become clear to me and that it would prove to be for my highest good.

Fortunately for me, I had woken up in the middle of the night a few weeks earlier with the feeling that I needed to check the sprinkler system in that building. I could recall a few details that came up during escrow but not much more. So I had a fire repair company go out and do some work on the sprinkler system to ensure it was working properly and met the requirements of the insurance company. After the fire, I called my insurance broker and the fire department in a state of total calm. The fire chief later estimated about $210,000 in damage to the burned-out, dark, lifeless, smoky, damp building.

I hung up the phone in the same state of total peace. I noted that the Robert from years past would have jumped into ass-kicking mode, taken a pound of flesh from everyone within a city block, and blamed everything on them. I would have left people hurt, confused, and feeling abused.

Instead, I had faith that this was happening for a reason and that it was for everyone's highest good. I held on to the belief that we are all unconditionally loved by Spirit, and I focused on learning whatever lessons I needed to as quickly, completely, and easily as I could, then I would be done. I would have new skills with which to embrace life, and I would be rewarded with a period of calm before I got my next lesson. I knew if I failed to learn these lessons now, they would keep coming back, stronger and stronger, until I finally learned them. It became clear that one of the lessons I needed to learn was to surrender. I believed that I didn't need to have all the answers and that God would help and guide me.

Over the next week, I spent time interviewing various remediation companies that handled burned buildings. It was obvious to the most casual observer that this was a very big project and a great deal of work needed to be done. Getting the building up to code would be no small task. Because the building was so old, it contained lead-based paint under the existing latex paint; it also had asbestos in the walls and roof. In all, repairs would include new roof, electrical, siding, flooring, walls, heaters, some windows, and two-thirds of the foundation. By the time all the repair work was done, the building would be virtually brand-new—and my insurance would cover the cost. The insurance also covered the lost rental income during the renovation and for a full thirty days after its completion (but because people weren't living in the building, I didn't have the usual costs of operation like electricity, water, repairs, phone service, cable, and onsite management fees). I was blessed with a professional, competent contractor who kept everything moving along smoothly. By the time everything was finished, the insurance settled with a payment of more than $623,000 for the building and $170,000 for a year of lost rental income.

The only threat of lawsuit that came as a result of the fire was from a lady who was not even a tenant of mine. Her case was quickly dismissed, and I paid only a $500 deductible.

That's not all: because the building had now been restored so beautifully to historic standards, it would receive a historical designation when the renovation was completed, which would enable me to qualify for a tax break every year as well as attract new quality tenants.

As mentioned in an earlier chapter, things don't always happen on our schedule. We may need to learn another lesson before something we desire can happen. It's like trying to get a flower to bloom before it's ready. No amount of additional sunlight, water, or fertilizer will make that happen. In fact, giving the bud too much of any of these three items can kill it.

So what do you do while you're waiting?? You surrender, exercise patience, and open yourself to whatever Spirit reveals to you.

Surrendering—letting go of the outcome—actually helps move things along. When you surrender, you'll have freed up time to focus on gratitude. When you surrender, you open yourself to the lessons Spirit has for you so that you can move along in your spiritual evolution.

"A map says to you. Read me carefully, follow me closely, doubt me not…I am the earth in the palm of your hand."

~ *Beryl Markham*, Pilot, Author,
West with the Night

Chapter 13

Setting Intentions

I was in the process of buying a thirteen-unit building in the Golden Hills area of San Diego when I decided it was time to see what would happen if I introduced some spiritual concepts into this part of my business. It's one thing to read and talk about these concepts, but they don't do any good until you put them into practice. It was time for the rubber to meet the road, as the old saying goes.

I arrived at the property driving my Prius instead of an exotic car. I was dressed in blue jeans rather than a suit. I was with my broker instead of my attorney this time. All of these things signaled that I was approachable and genuinely wanted to make things work for everyone's good.

I walked up to the owner, smiled, and shook his hand. After some brief introductions, the owner began the tour. I had already decided I wasn't going point out all the property's faults, as was my usual practice. Instead,

as we walked the property, I mentioned the things that I liked about it. Each time I mentioned something I liked, the owner gave me a surprised look. (It was like he was thinking, *What planet is this guy from*?) I could tell he took great pride in his buildings, and with each positive comment I made, he seemed to relax a little bit more. Rather than criticize, I pointed out how I might be able to increase the cash flow and make the property more profitable.

During the tour, I noticed that both the buying and the selling brokers were stressed out and restless. This was a relatively large transaction, and I knew they wanted it to go through. While we were there, a tenant randomly drove up to give the owner the keys to the unit she had vacated. She hugged the owner, and they talked for a minute. In my twenty-two years of buying and managing properties, I had never seen a tenant embrace a landlord. I noticed that the brokers were watching this all unfold as well.

I turned to my broker and said, "You never hug me!" Everyone started laughing. My broker grabbed me and gave me a big bear hug. Then everyone started hugging each other. It was a love fest right there behind the building. The mood was instantly elevated, and everyone continued the tour with big smiles on their faces. I silently laughed as I wondered how this transaction was going to end if it was starting like this.

After we walked the property, I told the owner that I liked his property. I said I wanted this deal to go smoothly and that I intended to handle any potential challenges with grace and ease. I know he had never before heard that expression, and he was still reeling from some of the compliments I had made. I even let him know that if we were not able to make a deal, it was okay; I had a friend who might be interested. I made it clear it was my hope that he find the absolute best buyer for his property. At this point, I again highlighted what I liked about the property. I let him know what improvements I would make in the first six months to get the rents up and preserve the building for the long term.

I asked the owner what was important to him, since he was offering owner financing. He shared that he wanted his asking price and needed to know that the property would be taken care of since he would be carrying the paper. He was asking for about 30 percent ($400,000) down, and I told him that I was willing to give him his asking price if he was willing to be flexible on the amount of money he required as a down payment. I suggested that we structure the loan into two loans with different interest rates. He would get the rate he wanted on his first; on the second, he would get a higher interest rate if he was willing to put more money into the deal via a lower down payment. I told the seller I wanted him to feel comfortable with me, and I was willing to open up my books to him. I told him he could look at any of the properties and individual units I owned to see that they were well maintained. I went a step further and told him he could talk to any of my investors about their experiences with my company and me.

The seller took a few days to think things over. He came back to me offering to reduce the down payment to 20 percent of the asking price, as I had requested—which is unheard of in that kind of seller's market. When I got the call saying he had agreed to my terms, I just sat staring out the window in amazement. If I had ever wanted independent confirmation that handling a transaction in a different way was going to produce more abundance, I had just received it. I remember thanking God with all my heart.

At the closing, the seller told me he was so impressed with the way I handled the transaction that he wanted to invest some additional money with me. He offered me more than $600,000. Using the principles of spiritual psychology in business proved a better way to do business, hands down. It was a win-win on so many levels. The transaction required less time and energy than my old way of doing business, I was able to raise additional capital, I made a friend, and I handled the transaction in a way that created less stress in my life. It was also a clear demonstration of what is possible with grace and ease.

This transaction also taught me a valuable lesson about abundance. Rather than piss off the owner by trying to grind him down on the price, get him to fix every imperfection in the building, and nitpick him on every detail, I nurtured a relationship. Both his heart and his pocketbook remained open. As a result, he had reduced the down payment and offered money for future transactions as an investor—which translated into even greater opportunities to change the way business was done.

"In my journey, I have learned that obstacles are opportunities. Acknowledge the obstacles and DON'T give them power."

~ *Vernice Armour* "FlyGirl",
1st African American Female Combat Pilot

Chapter 14

Be Impeccable with Your Word

Investors are a critical part of any business. Without capital, businesses can't grow. Banks often play a part, but their tolerance for risk is limited, and they are bound by changes in the economy, government regulations, and financial trends. Getting a loan under the first and second Bush administrations was the equivalent of fogging a mirror—if you were breathing, you could get a loan. That's rarely the case anymore for those who want to buy real estate.

That makes being impeccable with your word more important than ever. It's a concept introduced by Don Miguel Ruiz in his book *The Four Agreements*. It simply means doing what you say you are going to do—no matter what, even if no one is looking. It won't always be easy or fun, but it is critical. And it's not so much a matter of what others will say if you don't keep your word—it's about what *you* will say about yourself.

I had put together a simple cash-flow analysis on a property I wanted to buy. I compared cash going in and cash coming out to determine if the investment made financial sense. When doing my calculations, I forgot to figure in the cost of building some storage sheds on the back of the property to provide more storage space for tenants. Sheds are a great way to add value to a property. They cost only $1200 each to build, and they can be rented out for $35 to $75 dollars a month, depending on the location. We had built eight of them, so my cash-flow calculations were off by about $10,000.

Before I went to the investor to explain the situation, I thought about how many times contractors had come to me to break the bad news—usually that the job had cost more than predicted and they were going to need more money if I wanted the job done right. They'd say they were sorry and that they would normally cover the difference but that cash was really tight. And if I couldn't make up the difference, suddenly I was the bad guy, because they had families to support. I would be left with an unfinished project. Every time I hear somebody even starting to go in that direction, the hair on the back of my neck stands up. I decided I was not going to do that to anyone. I was going to be impeccable with my word.

I went to the investor and explained the error. I also told her I was going to use my own $10,000 to make the problem right. Mia was so impressed with my level of integrity that she went on to become my highest-dollar investor and a trusted friend. It cost me $10,000 to keep my word, but I made way more than that as a result in the years that followed. Now when we do a deal I call Mia up, discuss the details of the transaction, and she wires me the funds the next day, before the paperwork has even been completed. Our level of trust has grown to the point where she knows I have her covered and that our relationship is the most important thing to me.

"There is no sport equal to that which aviators enjoy while being carried through the air on great white wings."

~ *Wilbur Wright*

Chapter 15

Nurture Yourself

Conventional wisdom says that if you're really serious about getting ahead, you will power through any issues that arise so you can get to the desired destination more quickly. You think that all you need to do is work more and demonstrate the strength of your will, and things will improve. You may have to work through the night or work every weekend for the next three months, but applying more time to the problem *should* resolve it, right?

It's a popular philosophy, but I disagree with it. I've proven in my own life that it's very possible to work less and achieve more. By taking time off and nurturing yourself, you come back to task refreshed and able to be more resourceful as you tackle any challenges that arise. You've probably had the experience of working hard to solve a problem only to find that the answer just "came" to you after a good night's sleep. When we are refreshed in body, mind, and soul, we function far

better than when we are exhausted from months of hard work and stress.

Self-nurturing is perhaps one of the most important concepts you will read about in this book—and it's also the simplest. Self-nurturing is an act of self-care that feeds you on emotional, intellectual, spiritual, and physical levels.

Emotional nurturing happens when you take time to play with your pet, kiss your mate, hug a friend, write a letter telling a family member how much you love them, or apologize to a coworker for the way you spoke to her. And here's the best part: while you are nurturing yourself by doing these things, you are also nurturing others.

Intellectual nurturing involves following an intellectual pursuit that you enjoy. For some, doing a crossword puzzle is both relaxing and stimulating to the intellect. For others, it may be learning a new software application or a new language, learning how to fly a plane, or assembling a bookshelf.

Spiritual nurturing may include meditating, praying, reading a spiritual text, volunteering your time at a shelter, sitting in silence, or taking a walk in nature and feeling gratitude for your life.

Physical nurturing might include getting a massage or facial, eating a healthy meal, sleeping in, or going to the doctor for your annual checkup. Don't underestimate the importance of physical nurturing: Your body is the temple of your soul, and you have it for just a short time. Love it unconditionally.

One thing I do well is vacation. In the past three years, I have flown myself to thirty countries while simultaneously growing my business. When I return from these vacations, I come back feeling invincible. I've spent hours on end relishing the silence and allowing all the distractions to just dissolve away. I am finally get free from all the endless chatter of my everyday life and can listen to what it is that I need. Here is a quote from my book, *Zen Pilot*, that details how nurturing flying can be: "After a bumpy ride with precipitation hitting the windshield at more than 200 miles per hour, I broke through the clouds to find the brilliant sun shining on a solid sea of the fluffiest white clouds imaginable. Thirty miles in the distance I could see a perfectly clear sky as far as my eye could see. At times like that, I knew I was loved unconditionally and all that was unfolding just for me."

There will always be a reason to not go on vacation—things will always come up in your life at the last minute. You'll need to get a report done. You'll get a big pimple that will be a joke on the beach. You'll feel guilty about leaving your dog, who suffers from separation anxiety. Forget all that and go. Just go. All those issues will be waiting for you when you get back, and you'll be much better able to handle them.

A great example of this is when I was planning a month-long solo flight into Alaska and eventually over the Bering Sea to Anadyr, Siberia. At the time, my house was costing me $10,000 a month in mortgage, taxes, repairs, and insurance. I was hemorrhaging cash at a

fantastic rate with that house, which I had been unable to sell or rent, and I wasn't happy about incurring the additional expenses of my planned flight. I meditated over whether I should go, and the response from Spirit in the silence was, "Just go."

I decided I was going to listen to Spirit on this one, no matter what. I was going to follow through on nurturing myself, and I was going to go on my vacation. For the first time in three and a half years, I totally let go of the outcome and honestly didn't care what happened with the house. I was not going to be held prisoner by the house, and I was confident that Spirit had my very best interests at heart. No more lying in bed at night worrying.

My house rented a week later.

Now arrangements had to be made quickly. I needed to be out of my house and in a new place before leaving on my vacation in two weeks. Funny how something can resolve itself effortlessly when it's meant to be, with Spirit at the helm. I had lunch that day with a buddy of mine from my military days who had just moved into a new house in Rancho Santa Fe. As it turns out, he had a small guesthouse and offered me its use. This additional synchronicity was a clear sign to me that I was in alignment with Spirit. I knew my belongings would be secure, and I could relax while I was gone without incurring a large debt.

But I didn't yet quite have my happy ending. To compound my challenges/lessons, an offer I had put in on a twenty-eight-unit building was accepted, and seven refinances I had going were due to close while I was away. If ever I had a reason to stay in town it was then. I considered cancelling the trip and taking care of business, but I was intent on nurturing myself with my planned vacation. I decided to go through with my plans, even though getting everything handled seemed impossible.

I asked for Spirit's help and had faith that everything would be fine. I trusted that Spirit—my twenty-four-hour-a-day business consultant—had given me guidance that was accurate and for my highest good.

I remember landing in Nome, Alaska, on a rainy day. No one else was in sight, and I wondered how I was going to pull all this off in a small town out in the middle of God's country. I was standing on a wet, sandy, dirty taxiway with mud all over my plane, wondering if I would even be able to get the plane back on the runway. I needed to leave for Russia the next day, and I had many things I needed to do before I left—including signing eight loan documents I didn't even have yet.

I walked into the only bank in town and asked if they had a notary on staff. As luck (or Spirit) would have it, a notary was standing next to me in line. She told me she had the fastest Internet connection in town and that she just so happened to have time available that day. A tremendous sense of calm washed over me. I was in alignment and being guided for my highest good. It didn't matter where on the planet I was, my connection to Spirit was clear, and my next steps were unfolding in front of me in perfect synchronicity.

It may have been tempting to ask myself, "Is it all worth it?" Maybe my challenges were an indicator that I shouldn't take the trip after all. Maybe Spirit was trying to prevent me from putting myself in harm's way. Maybe I was going to run out of fuel over the Bering Sea and crash in the frigid waters off the coast of Siberia.

Let me assure you that the trip was well worth it. It was one of the most profound things I've ever experienced, and it changed my life in so many ways. It made clear to me that Spirit was always with me—always guiding me, always loving me unconditionally. I learned from this experience that life is for me to live and learn and that I am an integral part of this planet.

One of the greatest things I learned was that nurturing myself is crucial if I want to grow and thrive. The same thing applies to you. When you neglect an opportunity to nurture yourself, you lose productivity and miss opportunities to live and learn. And perhaps most importantly, when we are open and connect to what Spirit has for us in the silent self-nurturing, we can trust that what is happening is for our highest good.

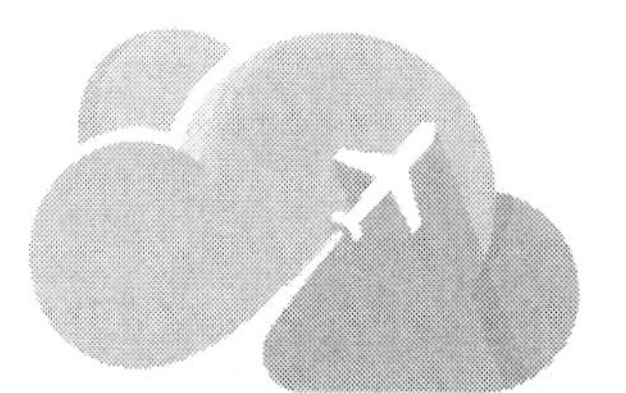

"Though it was a place where I could quickly die, the cockpit was a place where I truly lived."

~ *Brian Shul*

Chapter 16

Reframe

Reframing simply means seeing things from another perspective. Often, the story you first tell yourself about a situation is driven by your fears and frames the situation in a less-than-desirable way. If you then slap some judgment on it, you would certainly label the situation as "bad."

If you carry that kind of energy, you might see yourself as the victim. You perceive that you're getting the raw end of the deal; you're convinced that the universe is conspiring against you. But that's rarely true. When you take the time to look at situations like this from a different perspective, things often become much more clear—and much closer to reality.

A great example involved my least enjoyable part of being a landlord—dealing with tenant evictions. When a tenant stopped paying rent in the past, I always perceived it as an intentional and premeditated attack on my business. I figured the tenants were living on my property, using my utilities, doing damage to my unit, yet breaching their written agreement with me. They were not being impeccable with their word, and that infuriated me. I felt powerless to do anything. The tenants were stealing from me and getting away with it.

The evictions kept me up at night and brought on anxiety attacks. I'm embarrassed to admit that I would sometimes call the tenants late at night and hang up on them. One time I even recorded the sound of gunshots off the Internet and played it into the phone. I often crept over to the building and turned off their hot water heaters so they had to wake up to a cold shower.

I figured if they were going to keep me up at night and mess with my world, I would do the same to theirs. Fighting fire with fire sounded like a reasonable way to operate; I was engaged in a "rental jihad" with those tenants. And let me assure you that getting tenants evicted is a time-consuming, involved, difficult process, even though *they're* the ones who've broken their agreement.

When I finally got these tenants to move out, I'd call them and vent my hostility by screaming at them, calling them every nasty name I could think of. It was my way of trying to release the rage I carried that was tearing me apart. I knew the upset and anger was poison to me, and I figured I needed to get it out rather than let it fester inside me. I was like a time bomb that was ready to explode at anytime—and I often did.

After spending countless hours on evictions, both in court and in my head, I decided it was time to reframe.

Maybe some compassion for everyone—including myself—was in order.

To start, I realized that 99 percent of tenants pay their rent if they possibly can. They don't want to be thrown out on the street. Chances are good that someone who fails to pay rent is already struggling with many other problems and doesn't want to add eviction to the list. I realized that I was scared, but so were the tenants. They needed to get something going fast, or they and their families were going to suffer.

I got a huge download from Spirit and help in reframing when I realized that this was never really about me. The tenants were not intentionally trying to hurt me or my business. That was an irrational thought I had been carrying around. I was playing the victim, and I needed to move away from that. I needed to demonstrate compassion for others—my tenants—who were trying to learn one of their lessons in life.

I stopped to really look at the actual situation. By the time an eviction was in progress, the lesson was being delivered in the form of a two-by-four across the head of both me and the tenant. The lesson had not been received the first few times the universe sent it out. It probably started with a late notice on one of the tenant's bills, then maybe the tenant's phone got shut off. Then the tenant was perhaps embarrassed when a friend found out the tenant got a "three-day notice to pay rent or quit." Now it had become a major issue because something needed to change in their lives. When I could see this situation for what it was—an

opportunity to learn—it made my conversations with my tenants much easier. I had reframed the situation.

When I reframed things, it totally changed the way I dealt with eviction. I met with the delinquent tenants and listened to what they had to say, holding a place of compassion for them. The conversations allowed the tenants to be heard and let them express the challenges they were experiencing. I repeated back what they told me so that I was clear on what they were saying and experiencing. I let them know that they had been good tenants and told them I knew they would be paying their rent if they could.

Once I heard everything they had to say, I shared my position and concerns. I told them I was also experiencing challenges as a result of this situation. I explained that I had commitments to the bank and investors, so I needed them to pay their rent; otherwise, my business couldn't function, and it affected many other people. I needed them to move out and go stay with friends until they got their feet back on the ground. I told them that if they handled this situation with integrity and honesty, I would consider taking them back once things settled down for them. I also made it clear that if they did not move out, eviction was my only option, and I would need to hire an attorney to get them out as quickly as possible. I explained that my company had a legally binding agreement and that we would enforce the terms and conditions of that agreement. I carefully explained that if they were evicted, it would affect their credit and cost several thousand dollars more in the long run.

Some tenants responded positively to this conversation and moved out. Others decided to wait it out. They were the ones who chose to fight the current of life and make their lessons in life much harder. They were missing an opportunity to learn with grace and ease. At that point, I had done everything I could do, and the situation was out of my control. I then called the attorney and let things go. I had accepted that in my business there were times when things like this could not be avoided.

There is another important business lesson here that my mentors have pointed out over the years. Every business includes things that are extremely challenging. If you can hire these parts out to people who are better suited to handle them, you can stay in a place of equanimity.

In my reframe, I realized that no one was intentionally trying to hurt me or my business. Rather, I realized that people occasionally encounter tough times—and in those times they do the best they can with the tool set they have. By seeing the situation with compassion, I avoided judging both delinquent tenants and myself.

"Our passionate preoccupation with the sky, the stars, and a God somewhere in outer space is a homing impulse. We are drawn back to where we came from."

~ *Eric Hoffer*

Chapter 17

The Energy Bubble

Sometimes life just seems unbearable. At times like these, you might wonder how you are going to survive from one moment to the next. You know that nobody can stand in for you. There are things you must simply do on your own. In moments like these, your strength seems to be tested, and you pray for the difficult times to end.

I want to share a technique that I have successfully used to get me through a few of these situations. It's called the energy bubble.

I was in sitting in superior court across from one of my tenants who was appealing a decision in my favor from small-claims court. She was furious and was accompanied by her mother, who had cosigned on her lease and therefore also had some liability. We could never satisfy this tenant. It was pretty clear to me that she was going to throw everything she had at me, including making disparaging remarks about me, my company, my workers, and anything else she could come up with. To complicate matters, the judge was getting so old that he had become totally unpredictable. Nobody had told me the circus was in town, but I found myself in the front row, and the greatest show on earth was about to begin!

I know this sounds a little "out there," but I decided I would surround myself with an energy bubble. I envisioned an impenetrable bubble of light around me. The tenant frantically tried to get at me, but I envisioned her just bouncing back. She made several attempts, but it was no use. She simply wasn't getting in. I felt compassion for her as someone who was lost and hurting. Misguided and angry, she had some work to do, just like all of us. Her issues were playing out with me, and there was no stopping them. We obviously had a contract to fulfill together.

I remember looking into her eyes and seeing sheer rage. She was furious. Her face was red, she was sweating, the tone of her voice was harsh, and if not for the laws that protect us, I'm sure she would have hit me. I was clearly getting more than what I could have humanly been responsible for.

After lots of intense yelling, finger pointing, accusing, and disparaging remarks, the court case ended favorably. Even though the judge was not completely rational, even he could see how calm I was and how irrational she was. After the judge gave his verdict, my attorney said that she had never seen anybody stay as calm as I had through such an all-out attack. I just smiled at her. I knew the things this tenant had said were not true. I knew I was in integrity.

As my attorney and I walked from the courtroom, I faced one more challenge. The tenant's husband was standing right in front of the door with his arms out. The veins on his forehead and arms were bulging, displaying his prison tattoos; he appeared to be in an attack stance. He was ready to fight. In order to provoke me, he called me a profane name. I remained calm and centered. I turned to my attorney and winked and smiled at her as we walked away.

That wasn't just a victory in court—it was a victory in life, because I succeeded in not getting upset. I didn't let someone's comments ruin my day as I would have in the past. It wasn't a "bad" experience but rather a wonderful learning experience to be remembered.

From that day on, I knew I could create an "energy bubble" wherever and whenever I needed one. The bubble was of course Spirit, once again demonstrating that I was unconditionally loved and showing me there was a way for me to remain loving.

Try it out sometime. It takes much less energy than getting upset.

"What are we doing here? We're reaching for the stars."

~*Christa McAuliffe*, Astronaut

Chapter 18

Overcoming Fear and Making Magic

One of the greatest barriers to growth is fear, the dark cloud that looms in your mind. Fear tells you what you can't do. Fear affects how you see the world. Fear comes and goes whenever it wants.

Fear can have such a grip on you that it directs you away from what you truly want in life. And to make matters worse, many are afraid to deal with fear.

As a pilot who flies over oceans, deserts, and mountains in a single-engine piston aircraft by myself, I deal with fear on a regular basis. When people ask me if I'm afraid, they seem surprised when I respond, "Hell, yes! Flying can be some scary shit!" Once they figure out that I'm mostly joking, I explain that fear is what keeps me alive.

When I started to learn how to fly, I promised myself and God that I would fly every two weeks. I knew that was the minimal requirement for staying sharp and alive. I start to get a little slower after two weeks of being in the cockpit nonstop. It takes me longer to find w looking for. If I need to locate the outside air temperature because I'm getting to an elevation where I may start to accumulate ice on the prop, leading edges, and windshield, it may take me a second longer to locate where it is displayed on the digital display. That extra second can be critical when flying any aircraft.

When feeling fear, I experience it in my stomach and in my mind. It usually starts with knots and butterflies in my stomach, followed by shortness of breath and my mind creating a novel about all the possible things that could happen to me and my passengers. I think about the level of responsibility I have for the other souls who fly with me.

Next, I feel a bit nauseated, and the little voice in my head I've named "Freddy Flier" starts to tell me stories. They go something like this: "You are not safe." "You are going to get yourself killed." "You are not a good pilot." I invite Freddy in and let him know I'm flying to be safe and that we need to work past this fear together. I tell him that I love him unconditionally and appreciate what he does for me.

If I don't let the fear in, I'm using up valuable energy to fight it by not allowing the natural process to work as God has intended. When I do let it in, it gets stronger for a time but then it dissipates. I need to honor the feelings that surface, give them a voice, feel them, and then let them go after I thank them for what they have taught me.

Flying is very much about overcoming your fears. Every pilot deals with fear in some form, and every pilot knows the sheer exhilaration that comes from overcoming that fear. To be free of your deepest fears is liberating. With each fear you overcome, you let go of one of the rocks you carry in your backpack. Those rocks are the things that keep you from soaring.

Some of the things that cause me fear may seem silly to someone else. I used to be terrified to click that little black mike button and say what I needed to say as quickly and precisely as possible using aviation parlance to communicate with the air-traffic controllers. I knew that every pilot within twenty miles was listening carefully, and if I screwed up I would be the topic of aviator stories for a very long time. And that's not all: I was talking to an air-traffic controller with years of experience who had no patience or time for dealing with beginners. Air-traffic controllers face the difficult task of managing many planes flying simultaneously at hundreds of miles an hour, filled with hundreds of souls.

As a landlord, I am terrified when I have to talk with angry tenants—even more terrified than I am of talking to air-traffic controllers. I don't like the energy that comes up and the things that are said that can't be taken back. When I'm called a name like "slumlord," it's just like saying that I don't care and haven't put my heart and soul into my work. I have taken these conversations very personally over the years, and I find them hurtful. My property business is one of my passions and represents a solid twenty-plus years of my life, during which time I've fought, sacrificed, suffered, and endured a number of difficulties to make it what it is. I delegate as much responsibility for dealing with tenants as I possibly can. But when a lawsuit is threat-

ened, I need to jump in and take the driver's seat. I am 100 percent responsible.

I have realized that the fear I experience is a service to my continuing evolution and well worth the energy it takes to overcome. After all, why would I want to carry it around with me everywhere I go? Why would I want to see the world through this filter? Imagine how different your world would be if you saw *everything* from a perspective of fear. It would be terrifying. One time, in dealing with a particular tenant, a thought popped into my head. *Why not overcome the fear of dealing with my tenant as I have overcome fear so many times in my plane?* If I could be fearless in my plane, I could be fearless in my business as well. I decided to reframe my fear and see the situation not as a challenge but as a learning opportunity. I decided to see it not as a situation where my company, my independent contractors, and I were being criticized but rather given an opportunity to improve the business. I decided to view each tenant call as if a consultant were calling to make some suggestions on how we could improve the business.

In one situation we were getting complaints that a particular tenant had visitors at all hours of the night, something that was disruptive to the other tenants. We had suspected drug activity for some time, but drug activity is difficult and expensive to prove in an eviction case. The tenants were frequently late with their rent and were carrying an outstanding balance from the past. We had some occasional theft on the property but were unable to tie it to any individual unit. It was just easier to ignore the problem, since this particular tenant eventually paid the rent and since it's not unusual for tenants to have conflicts with their neighbors.

I finally realized I was living with a knot in my stomach over this issue and that it was not going to go away. I occasionally woke up in the middle of the night feeling anxiety and fear. I realized that it was time to deal with this issue directly and overcome my fear. Our conversations trying to persuade the tenant to leave were unproductive, so we were forced to file an eviction.

At that point, the situation got worse. Late-night activity increased, and rent payments stopped altogether. The crime rate on the property skyrocketed, and we had some undesirables hanging around. Eventually the problem tenants left before their case came to court. Despite some major renovation costs and the preliminary eviction cost, we got the property under control. The crime rate went to zero, there were no more calls from complaining tenants, and the knot in my stomach disappeared. We learned from this situation. We decided to start inspecting all units quarterly and to act more aggressively on any tips we received.

As I reflect on this situation, I see the blessing in what transpired. That initial complaint and the challenging work that followed forced my buried fear to the surface so I could heal it. What greater gift could we get from another person than to help us evolve?

Your ability to turn any situation into a positive in just an instant is absolutely magic. And when that happens, something you feared turns out to be something terrific. And there's not much better magic than that.

"When once you have tasted flight, you will forever walk the earth with your eyes turned skyward, for there you have been, and there you will always long to return."

~ *Leonardo da Vinci*

Chapter 19

Tying It All Together

Hopefully you have learned some powerful spiritual principles in this book, which you can apply in your life and in your business. But I need to clarify an important point: informed decisions can't be based on spirituality alone. There are some pretty spiritual people who are barely functioning in the real world. You and I and everyone else on earth have real-world realities we need to deal with every single day. And that's why I've shared my real estate experiences in conjunction with spiritual concepts.

I'd like to share a story that illustrates how real-world experiences and spirituality work together.

One day my best friend from childhood called me unexpectedly on my cell phone. When he called, I was at Squaw Valley on a self-nurturing retreat as a reward for a busy couple of months. We hadn't spoken for at least five years. He asked how I was doing, and I let him know how well things were going for me. I had just bought two properties at the same time, which often

happens at the end of the year when people need to sell their properties for tax reasons. Most buyers are busy with the holidays, creating a unique situation of more sellers than buyers.

When I asked my friend how he was doing, he replied, "Not well."

Bill was about to lose custody of his daughter and two properties due to an ugly divorce he was going through. He had gained a considerable amount of weight, virtually doubling in size, and had developed sleep apnea. The first surgery his doctor attempted didn't resolve the sleep apnea, so they broke his jaw and reset it, hoping to clear his airway. He became addicted to the pain medication they gave him after the surgery. He lost his job, and his wife decided she wanted out as well. By the time he contacted me, he had spent more than $500,000 on attorney's fees. He needed $10,000 to hold on to his two properties.

Bill's situation was a clear case of what happens when we fight the current of life. Being at war with anyone, including yourself, *never* pays dividends. His conflict signaled a disconnect with Spirit and the beginning of a series of very intense lessons.

Bill caught me off guard, and I knew enough not to make a snap decision. I told him I needed a couple days to think about what I wanted to do. I got back to him after talking to some of my friends and mentors. I told him if his financial ship was sinking, I didn't want to go down with it; he should just let the ship go. He assured me that his financial ship was not sinking. In hindsight, my intuition was telling me not to lend him the money. In fact, as you are reading this you are probably saying, "No, don't do it!"

I did make the loan to him out of what I thought was compassion and family loyalty. In reality, I was acting as an enabler who prevented him from learning his lessons. I also threw most of my good business sense (wisdom and experience) out the window—but not all of it. I told him I wanted to take a lien on his two properties for $10,000 each. When he paid me off, I would remove the liens.

Bill made a couple of payments, and then he was gone. I made some calls to him but got no reply. I called Bill's brother and learned that Bill was in prison. When I researched the charges against him, I learned he had been committing medical insurance fraud and had gotten caught. Before coming to me, he had financially tapped out his family. I had been his last resort.

A few months later, Bill's brother Frank called me and asked me to remove the liens so they could save the properties. I told him I would be happy to remove the liens as soon as they paid me what they owed. I explained the liens were in place to protect my business interests. Frank told me they didn't have the money and asked if I would remove the liens as a favor to their family. I told him I had already done a favor for the family by lending Bill the money in the first place, and I was going to hold my ground.

I heard they lost one or both of their investment houses in foreclosure a short time later. Several years later, when Bill got out of jail, he contacted me and asked me not to fight his bankruptcy filing. I knew there had to be many other creditors in front of me, so I just let it go and never expected to see any money. At the time, I chalked it up to learning a valuable lesson with respect to doing business with friends; I knew that my attempt at compassion was overshadowed by a poor business decision.

I was saddened to hear that Bill had died about a year later. His death seemed a tragic end to a very sad experience for him and his family. Approximately ten years after I'd loaned Bill the money, I received a check in the mail from his mother for $10,000. In the letter that accompanied the check, she thanked me for standing by her family in their time of need.

I don't know whether the funds were repaid to remove the liens or to fulfill the family's commitment. That doesn't really matter. It *does* matter that keeping the liens was prudent in protecting my interest and recognizing a real-world reality. The funds were never truly mine. I was just holding them for a time and passing them along to bring about greater abundance and a change in the world. (I am investing the $10,000 in my Internet speaking platform and book in an attempt improve the lives of others.)

I hope you will share what you have learned in this book so you too can experience more abundance in your life as you have a positive effect on the world. My hope is that if each of us gives back—sharing wisdom, abundance, and experience—we will all experience a more Spirit-driven world.

So where are things today?

I found that the deeper I went into my spiritual transformation, the less interested I became in the material world. I saw myself as a soul having a human experience. I sold many of my personal belongings, including my exotic car, my collectable motorcycle, and my executive home filled with designer furniture. I moved into a small, quiet cottage in the country. I went from a forty-two-hundred-square-foot, three-story executive home with a view overlooking San Diego Bay to a five-hundred-square-foot studio cottage in the country. As I downsized, I focused on experiencing people rather than things.

In the silence that surrounds my country cottage, I focused my time on my spiritual studies. I began using more of my spiritual principles and practices in business and life, as I hope you will. As mentioned, I began to see explosive growth in all areas of my business. I started doing volunteer work at the San Diego Rescue Mission, a local homeless shelter, where I got to see how little one really needs to be happy. Food, clothing, shelter, medical care, love, and Spirit are all we really need. I found that life began to flow even faster and great things started to happen to me.

With respect to investors, I now have millions more investor funds than I can place in new properties. I find new investors all the time just by sharing authentically and talking about my passions. One evening, I was having dinner with some new friends who have done similar flying trips around southern Africa. When the conversation turned to business, flying, spirituality, and life, I spoke about these topics with the great passion I feel for each. I shared the lessons I have learned, and the abundance with which I have been rewarded. My new friend sitting next to me said that if I ever need some investor money for my business, to give him a call. I wasn't asking for an investor—I was simply talking authentically about my passions, being in alignment with Spirit, and expressing how I wanted this to be a better world for everyone. And the Universe showed me abundance yet again.

My relationships changed radically as well. For the first time in my life, relationships became my highest priority. When I asked Spirit for help in my relationship life, I thought about the three women with whom I felt I could be in a lifetime partnership. Within five minutes, all three had texted or e-mailed me. I had not heard from two of them in months. I later realized that Spirit was bringing up the issues I had with each of them so I could heal the pain/hurt and then attract a partner with whom I could go the distance.

The less I focused on money, the more money my business seemed to generate. When I let go of the outcome of making and keeping money, Spirit was rewarded me with the resources to go and pursue my passions of business, spirituality, and flying. Spirit wanted me to deepen these experiences so that I could share them with others. And the more I deepened them, the more I had to give and share with others.

Through it all, there is one constant: the learning doesn't stop. If anything, it accelerates. The lessons can be learned anytime, anywhere. We must constantly apply our tools, because we will be tested. I was reminded of this one summer during a three-week self-flight around five southern African countries with Susan Gilbert, my web designer, mentor, former business partner, occasional shrink, and lifetime friend. Our lessons started right where we'd ended things almost ten years earlier. I found that when circumstances became extreme and I was immersed in the daily stress of being a bush pilot in the "inhospitable" terrain of the African outback, in a plane with faulty parts, flying without weather reporting or traffic deconfliction, some of my new communication skills flew out the window and into the atmosphere—poof! The old "Bobby D Steamroller" came back for a brief cameo as I attempted to deal with corrupted airport officials, with much-needed fuel providers, and with my friend and copilot. I had studied so much and applied so much in my life, but Spirit continues to show me where I still have work to do.

When I returned to San Diego, I was caught up on my work in just a day and a half. I came back to 100 percent occupancy of my rental units, and the trip was already paid for. I was feeling relaxed—and aside from the differences in time zone, I began to dream again about what future adventures and lessons were in store for me.

A Final Thought

I want to thank you for spending your valuable time reading this book. It has been my profound and deepest pleasure to share these spiritual principles and

practices with you. I hope the stories I've shared will resonate with you and that you will practice what you learn every day. Would you like to stay inspired with the concepts and ideas I've shared with you here, long after you've closed the book and put it on the shelf?

I hope you said, YES!

And if so, I have a gift for you.

I've created a colorful Poster with

19 Tips for you to continue Flying Thru Life.

It's my gift to keep you inspired.

Print it out and hang it on your refrigerator, next to your computer screen, on your bathroom mirror – where ever you will see it regularly. Read the Trigger Tip Word and the inspiring explanation of that word or phrase.

Just go to:

www.FlyingThruLife.com/Awesome-Poster

If I can be of service to you, your organization, or a group that would like to hear more about any of these topics, please reach out to me at www.flyingthrulife.com. I would love to hear from you. Until then, I wish you a blessed life in which you fl ow with the current of life and achieve your personal and spiritual goals with grace and ease.

About the Author

Robert DeLaurentis loves to fly and loves to help people change with grace and ease through applied spirituality. He is a successful real estate entrepreneur and investor, pilot, speaker, author, and philanthropist. He has an undergraduate degree in accounting from the University of Southern California and a graduate degree in spiritual psychology with an emphasis in consciousness, health and healing from the University of Santa Monica. A Gulf War veteran, Robert served in the Navy for 14 years. After receiving his pilot's license in 2009, Robert has flown solo to more than 30 countries in the past three years and completed his first solo around the world trip in August 2015 visiting 26 countries in 90 days.

Robert finished Flying Thru Life shortly before embarking on his epic solo flight in his single engine Piper, Malibu Mirage. He is currently working on his second book, Zen Pilot.

He is available to speak to business groups, pilot organizations, personal and professional development conferences, non-profit fundraisers, schools, and youth groups. For more information on speaking engagements or media appearances, please contact him at:

http://www.FlyingThruLife.com/contact/

Made in the USA
San Bernardino, CA
13 September 2015